For a complete list of books by Coolgmack, as well previews of upcoming books and more info you can visit him or find him on Facebook, Instagram, twitter, snapchat, amazon.com, search for Coolgmack also you can find his musical soundtracks to his poetry on youtube.com

also check out coolgmack.com for books and merch
On coolgmack.com   coolgmack@gmail.com

Poetic Injustice$ In Amerikkka

By

Coolgmack

Published by coolgmack
With Coolgmack's Enterprise

Poetic injustices in Amerikkka by Coolgmack

Published by bookKing publishing

isbn # 978-1733680769
coolgmack.com

Copyright ©2022 coolgmack

All rights reserved. No portion of this book may be reproduced in any form without permission from the publisher, except as permitted by U.S. copyright law. For permissions contact: coolgmack@gmail.com

ACKNOWLEDGEMENTS

First and foremost, I would like to give thanks to God almighty. Without him rescuing me continuously I wouldn't be here writing this poetry. I might've been where the vultures eat or in some penitentiary beefing over a seat. But instead, I'm still standing. I would like to give thanks for my family that overstands my insanity and doesn't undermine my sincerity and lent a hand to me in my calamity. A special thanks goes to my core family that saw more of my galore vanity but still didn't underhand me or abandon me. Shout out to my day 1's since we were raised suns. my bro's Bolo, Coldcash, Goldy, Rico and Dollar that made sure they relayed their saved funds throughout my various incarcerations. Shout out to all my jail bidders that still didn't make it and to those that held their heads upstate and in the feds, even when they gave us nothing but water and bread in them oppressed staycations but still stuck to their pledge. Stay positive and have constant mental elevation and keep your mind guarded from Satan. Never give up your dreams of making it. The laws are changing, the flaws are erasing, never ever give up. the seeds need your vegetation, one day your time is coming up. Shout out to all the real ones in the feds who never took that cheese or crook their knees who stood tall through it all, you will never fall, don't turn into a patient but wait patiently. Shout out to all the racist cops and c.o's that thought you was teaching me lessons but instead were beseeching me blessings that enabled me to get these testaments. Those experiences only made me stronger and gave me the stability to endure longer through all your torture. Even though I never wronged ya. Thanks to all the childhood frenemies that used to tease me and told me I was fat and greedy. That motivated me to be healthy and now I give back and feed teens. Now I'm wealthy mentally and physically. Thanks to all the strangers that supported me financially and spiritually, I feel it in my spleen. Thanks to the people that I disrespected and accepted my apologies, that was not me. That was the drugs that turned me into bugged thug I swear solemnly. Shout out to everyone I know there's too many to name from the group home days and the drug game. I'm still the same, my coping skills just changed. a special thanks to all the libraries that gave me a safe place to create and a space to alleviate the hate from 8 to 8. Last but not least thanks for the alleged victim that lied on me, but indeed I was a menace to my society. So, you helped me change indirectly, when they put that 9 in me. I forgive you because God forgave me, I didn't get arrested, I got rescued from them crazy streets, sheesh!!! So, may God bless you. I wish the best for you. I could've, should've or would've been a vegetable, but somehow, I beet the odds without cheating the cards. That's my confessed truth. But now I'm with God and I can achieve, and succeeded thus far, because I believe in Allah. Thank God and thank y'all for taking the time out of your day to read these words on this page just to hear what I have to say… I appreciate you. Hopefully we can all see a change.

Disclaimer

To whom it may be concerned the purpose for this book is to stop the burns and for our tots to learn. For them to not return and to encourage them to yearn for a better turn and not be consecutively competitive to earn an urn. As I churn these words into vivid visions reminiscent of the horrid horrific predicaments that I was positioned in. Growing up in Amerikkka and being a citizen in a country that was different from what the textbooks was mentioning. The intellectual crooks were enforcing me to read so I could succeed in a school system that was missing the peace that I needed to achieve. They didn't teach me to be financially free independently without the GUV. My apologies. I was just a product of the streets. *But I am not a racist*!!! nor do I promote hatred towards Caucasian races that operated, and slave traded my ancestors and my generation. I'm just against injustices, it's just us against this racist systematic government, and the instilling of the willie lynches which is the linchpin to the white supremacy missions. It's US against THEM. Which THEM; can be members of any race that implements hate, so if it doesn't apply then let it fly and if it does then shame on you. It doesn't matter if you're black, white, blue, Asian or Spanish. I'm against whoever that promotes hatred and the action and the planning of it. The only way we can conquer this is with love, knowledge, wisdom, and understanding. It's 2022 we must come together to see the grey area and expand it. We shouldn't hate the next man or woman because of their skin blend. Whether we agree or disagree, we can at least agree to disagree and let's make this make sense. All lives can't matter if black lives aren't a matter. We must first reverse the hurt if equality is what we're after. We must endorse just enforcement in enormous proportions and of course get retribution for our losses to offset this awfulness. Education is the key. Don't blame me, I'm just a messenger who cares, prophesizing the truth here, something like a soothsayer, but this isn't a game, this is all truth and dares, the proof is clear like the last two years. I'm just helping my people with my 20-20 vision through the peephole, so we can be equal and won't see a sequel; Ezekiel 39:27 but I am not a reverend nor am I half stepping, this is my God's gifts and methods. *I am not a racist* I promote love over hatred and demote drugs for education. This is just my perception from the knowledge I ingested, and my personal experiences manifested, and this is directed to those that selected to infect us. This is for those affected by Amerikkka, God blessed US. The author assumes no responsibility or liability for any errors or omissions in the content of this project. The information contained in this book is provided on an intellectual basis with no guarantees of completeness, accuracy, usefulness, or timeliness. Enjoy, live, and learn from this, but do me one favor, let's not look back and turn into bricks. Like Lot's wife, let's use our God's given rights and that's the will to choose to live life just right. The material and information contained in this book is for general purposes only, you should not rely on content in this book as basis for making any irrational decisions homie.

TABLE OF CONTENTS

TABLE OF CONTENTS 8
SISTA LOVE!!! 1
QUEEN OF DIAMONDS 3
QUEEN OF CLUBS 7
QUEEN OF SPADES 11
QUEEN OF HEARTS --- PARTY ASTARTE 13
P.U.$.$.Y? 15
LOST AND TURNED OUT 19
LET'S REVERSE THE CURSE 23
MI$$ ME WITH THE BULLSPIT 25
IT WAS HER 29
    CHAPTER 2: HOPE 35
ART OF WAR 37
QUANTUM LEAPS 39
NEVER EVER QUIT 41
HOPE 43
DON'T DO IT! 47
NO HOPE IN DOPE 51
UNITY IN MY COMMUNITY 55
DEAR AMERIKKKA 57
COLD KNIGHTS 59
WILL YOU 61
2+2=4 63
FLAWS AND DISORDERS 65
PREY 4 FREEDOME 67
REVOLUTION SOLUTION 71
    CHAPTER 3: PAIN CHRONICLES 73
PAINGRY 75
I'M PAINGRY TOO!!! 77

URGENT CARE DOESN'T CARE!!!	81
MERRY XXXMI$$	83
HOSPITALITY	87
ME AND MY CANE	93
SORRY, I'M NOT SORRY	97
P.C.P	99
HUNGER PAINS	103
CHAPTER 4	107
PRICELE$$	109
C.O.P.	111
OPERATION LOCKDOWN	115
MIRACLE WHIP	119
NO RETREAT OR SURRENDER TO HIS HORRIBLE AGENDAS	121
GR8	123
REVOLT OR VOTE	125
RED WHITE AND THE BLUES	127
CHAPTER 5 BROTHER LOVE	131
HEY BLACKMAN	133
VETERAN'S DAY	137
MY MESSAGE TO THE BLACKMAN	139

RAISING SUNS 143

BLACK IS BLACK	147
BYRD IN THE AIR	149
JUDGE A JUDGE	151
CHAPTER 6: SCHOOL'S IN SU©©E$$ION.	153
WHO AM I?	155
WAKE UP!!!	159
WAKE UP NIGGAS!!!	161
STAY AWAKE!!!	163
REALIZE REAL LIES	165

SOULS4SALE	169
ARISE AND FLY	171
PICK YA POISON	175
DO BLACK LIVES STILL MATTER?	179
REAL E$TATE	181
WAKE UP EVERYBODY	183
HUEMAN	185
COCO B-AWARE	187
ADOLESCENT LESSONS	189
BAD NEWS	191
ABOUT THE SEXY AUTHOR	197

Chapter 1: Sista love♥

SISTA LOVE!!!

Any friendships or relationships that don't go through trials and tribulations may not be real in all reality. That's why I value principalities and qualities and don't let just anybody follow me. But I would love to embrace you because I'll know that you will succeed. But sis, I can never make you, you would have to want to believe. If she can achieve it. Then you can too! Surround yourself with a positive group that can grow into lucrative loops. You will do good in school because life is nothing but a college miss. Once you acknowledge them, learn from your burns then abolish them. Improvement is the biggest room so make sure your floors are polished with something meaningful to stand on. Go-get your goals and follow them. Never let them Freddy Kruger's kill your dreams, hone your talents sis. Matthew 25:23 Alyssa Thomas, Michael Jordan, show your resilience sis. You are a child of God. So, with yourself you got to be honest sis and take it one day at a time and nil them haters with a silence sis. Together we can overcome these police brutality violences and tackle these crooked policies. But it's going to be a challenge sis, to get thru the fallacies. We got to vote against the racist system; they're Willie Lynching US different sis. They pimping our minds but we're too blind and at a difference to see the differences. But sis, it's okay it's not your fault, both of our daddies were locked up north. Trapped inside them prison system corp$ with just their thoughts. They were supposed to give us support and teach us what their past ancestors taught, but they succumbed to the war on drugs that the government sought. They paid the cost of being wrought from the battles that were fought. Some played a sport, some chose to snort, while others chose to resort to Resorts. Others chose the fast life of crack pipes chasing highs from last night or the satisfaction of the cash hype that attracted more blacks than whites. Then the system replaced the black role models with these cell phones and attention-grabbing apps, no man in the house equals hell in the homes and the kids having naps. I know because I became one of them that got locked up instead of being a godly family man. Now I'm back to help you as much as I can because I care, and I understand. I was a buried gem inside that Candyland like crushed coal. Now I'm shining like a diamond, and I can enlighten you to what you must know. Together we can change the world like Phyllis Hyman and not be unwoke. The 1st two assignments are self-love and not at each other's throat. You can't love someone else in its entire sense without first loving yourself. Together we can save this environment but only with each other's help. I love you for the sake of Allah and by keeping his promises, I promise sis. To do the best that I can to help you understand what they're doing to US. I won't stop until I can accomplish it. We got this sis, there's nothing that can hold us back, there's no stopping us that's a fact. But I can't do this all by myself I need your help, your Sista love

QUEEN OF DIAMONDS

Keep ya head up sis

I know what you're going through.

Every day is another hustle

But you gotta do what you gotta do.

You're so amazing!!!

Raising kids on your own

Without government assistance
You been this way since you were grown

Homeschooling your children

When they come home from school

So, they don't get trapped in the trenches

And don't turn out to be a fool

You got several streams of income

So, you don't have to be dependent

On another man to get it from

You know how to get it

You're so terrific

You put God first, then family and goals

And avoid those that goes against it

Even when calamity hit your road

You knew how to smile through the blemishes

Even when the Plandemic hit

And you were facing that eviction

You still didn't quit

You never flinched, you're so resilient

That was never an option

When your back was against the wall

You saw a fence you chose to hop it

You stood tall, you were never meant to fall
You had to hustle like a Jamaican

Just so your kids can make it

Opportunities you had to take them

They didn't come if you were complacent

Like Mayweather you excelled youy greatest

When they tried to box you in

You didn't even have to get naked

Because that isn't the type of mom you is

You set good examples to your children

to embrace and take in

Instead of trying to get a million

You were striving to make great kids

Then you moved out the projects

Figuratively then physically

Armed your family like biceps

Literally and mentally.

You're a diamond in the rough,

I just want you to know that.

I'm so proud of you hun,

You never gave up, that's a whole fact

Queen Of Clubs

She's like a splash of a black cleopatra, an African Queen. She's from the essence like an actress or an activist from the black magazine. She's like a movie with the best scenes that you have ever seen. But her flesh isn't so fresh, and her message isn't so clean. She's an outcast casted out from the worldly normalcies. Her passion is fashion and you cannot fathom her majesty. Her fragrance is something you will never seem to forget. She's just a prodigy of her environment; her self-esteem is prestigiously affixed. Ever since she was a kid she was singing about illicitly working and twerking even before her brain was learning the significance behind the lyrics that she was blurting. Her future is uncertain because she's turning to her phone and her TV for guidance. Being silent is a challenge because her vaginal pH is imbalanced. Every day of the week is a different party. She mixes Percs with Bacardi, which is subconsciously reversing her health in her body. She doesn't even eat properly, her diet consists of liquor, fried chicken, and lots of weed. Which is also toxically ruining her relationship with her family obviously. But she doesn't see what she's doing, because she's blinded by the love of the money that she is pursuing. She's just a beauty, who uses her booty to get paid. She hides her eyes behind designer shades, so they don't give away what she's really trying to say. She's an independent woman but still lives with her momma, which is a safe haven from the piranhas. She hangs with the snakes and anacondas because it feels ill good and fulfills the bills for her Prada's. She wakes and bakes every day. That's just her way to escape from the drama and the realities of life. Her priorities aren't right. She has no self-respect and for the check she'll just do it like Nike. She dances around responsibilities at different nightclub facilities. She will respond to her needs after her wants are appeased. She's a top model on IG but her only fans pay her rental fees. Her Macy's booster shopping sprees have her wardrobe on fleek. Her main man of the week rotation is on repeat. Money talks; she deals with no Charlie Sheens; her conversations aren't cheap. She became anti-social because her circle wasn't in her corner when she needed them, because they were tired of the "I'll tries" and the lies that she was feeding them. She won't gain peace until she releases the chains that's enslaving her brain. It is never too late to embrace change and give God the reigns. Today she is still that queen, because it was God she believed in. She did an about face on the things that disabled her from succeeding. That enabled her to lead, to teach, to preach, and to reach higher heights. It was the sacrifice of her past life that made it all right. When she empathized and centralized in the passion of Christ. She started to realize that she had a life worth living past the strife. She started assisting other women in becoming a better woman. She understood then that you got to forgive to be forgiven. It became her power as she empowered those who followed her. As she rose like a flower and bloomed every room that she encountered. Her imperfections are accepted by the most respected God of the heavens, because of her repentance and her good intentions. She turned her lessons into blessings, and she will never forget them. Now she hardly parties because her life is different. She's in the gym working on her strength, her health is in a better condition.

QUEEN OF SPADES

All she cares about is the whereabouts of her children. She's dealing with stress and anxiety every time she exits her building. There's a variety of feelings that she's withholding on a daily basis, that keeps building, but you would rarely see it in her many faces. She keeps it basic and concealed in, she prays.... amen!!

She blends in like chameleons and stay away from strange men. She's not afraid, but she never strays from the ways that pay the rent. She doesn't switch from the makeshifts of what the day brings in. She's brilliant but also appealing. She's striving to raise a nation, with dreams of fulfilling a million fulfillments but with patience. She moves like a civilian in the field of independency. She strives with minimal government assistance because that isn't the way it was meant to be. She's resilient but anxiously praying for a victory. Her will is to see that her children make it back home from the streets in one piece. But the instant resistance they must go through is befuddling. With no relief in the streets, they seem to always be getting into trouble again. They must dodge the police, the beast, and the crooked policies. Which are systematically making them an opp they don't want to, but they got to be. As they step over the puddles in the streets from the reigns that's illogically keeping them constrained and confined to sovereignty poverty. A place obviously where their innocence must be proven not guilty, sheesh!!! Then proclaimed without blame that their chances to win are slimmer than the lottery. They will more than likely catch a DWB in these streets than to die from an airborne infectious disease honestly. Her only option for her seeds is that they got to achieve. So, she leans on Jesus honorably, so they can succeed more than probably. She pleads to possibly lead them out of this Plandemic season possibly. Life could be quite puzzling and obsequious without an apology, for no reason like the oddest odyssey. As she subconsciously sees demons in her mind as she sleeps. She keeps her children away from the swine and the fleas as she flees and tries not to lead them astray. She stays on the grind like coffee beans, in hopes that they don't see her dismay or the steps she's taking for her seeds to achieve as she's trying to right their wrongs. She has to be awakened at seven for her 9 to 5 that she's overqualified for. Yes, it's stressing and repetitive but it's all for a better living. She's a Queen so she'll make a way for her children to eat every Thanksgiving. She won't stop striving, as she is trying to find her inner peace. The thesis of her mind which was once broken, now is in one piece. She is more focused and knows that she was chosen to lead. She no longer wears her hopes on her sleeves; her emotions are on freeze. Like a rose at its peak, she knows she is valuable and bonafide and worth more than a whore or any toy that a boy can buy. But she accepts their gifts with an awkward eye. Her thoughts are to the sky. When she walks her thighs.... move with determination. She's determined to make it without having to get naked. The chains she's got to break them. The mayhem, and the barriers that society has been making. She knows her worth, and her work isn't worth the tolls that they are taking. But she decides to put her pride to the side and ride, to do what she got to do for her boo and her two little guys. She's a queen that's crowned by the almighty King, as she accepts responsibilities for her being, she's free.

QUEEN OF HEARTS --- PARTY ASTARTE

Wow… how… have…. all of these…
Young, black, brown, white, queens…. Gone missing???
Out of their households some are as young as 12yrs old. It isn't solely of them being promiscuous. It's sad to see that at age of fifteen, to have to grow up in these conditions. Getting robbed of their dreams, hopefully they can start using their loss as an ambition. Being almost forced into a position to be an adult with no supervision can be hard to deal with infliction. Growing up in broken homes. Every day the super is in the kitchen fixing himself a plate on the dirty dishes while the neighbor's listening. All I see on FB and IG is these enhanced booty beautiful women indirectly teaching their kids how to be prostitutes, hoes, and bit%hes, no

disrespect if you're offended. At a young age they're seeing you busting it open for the Benjamins. Wining and dining with different men, smoking weed and cigarettes. They watch what you say and watch what you do and when they grow up, who you think they want to be? Just like you. I hope you don't feel disrespected or get my poem misconstrued. I'm not your critic, I'm just a messenger that came to speak the truth. I can see that you're not approachable, I just hope you can see the proof. I hope this goes deep in your roots and grows into a tree full of fruits. There are these racist scientists out there doing all those experiments, and there's too many missing kids. I just hope we can tie the loose ends. It seems like the further we grow apart, the weirder it gets. They want us divided so that we can be conquered. That cat shouldn't have a price tag attached to it, it should be honored. But there's nothing wrong with making yourself more valuable, but not for the highest bidder. No, I'm not bitter, just here to empower you. It shouldn't take just a hundred dollars or two to deflower you. But believe me, I'm no better than you, I used to allow it too. Thank God I lived to regret it. I'm sorry I hope my apologies are accepted. Besides your worth more than a check, you should be more respected. But it must start with yourself. You can't party away your health and expect others to see a positive effect on your results. I'm just a poetic messenger telling you how I felt when I see a girl selling their soul for fool's gold that could melt. I love you like my sister, even though we're not related physically. We are family because we got the same father in heaven spiritually. Together we stand divided we fall, hand to hand we can right the wrongs.

P.U.$.$.Y?

P u s s why!!!
Do you want me to treat you like a prostitute?
I rather empower you because I see more value in you.
But I guess that you're used to them other foreign dudes.
They just want to come through to deflower you.
What's wrong with you?
I would rather salvage you and be on the side of you.
Spitting knowledge to you, not devouring you.
Helping you get through these tough times to get ahead, advising you. Instead of giving you that molded bread you'll rather me to provide to you.
To me, you're worth more than a green paper that's unreliable,

with a slave master posing on that I can slide to you.
You shouldn't view what God gave to you, as a price tool.
You're worth more than you're asking me to pay for,
Are you high boo?
I'm being more than nice to you.
I hope you take my advice too.
It's not only because I adore you, but I really do like you.
I never met anyone else, that was just quite like you.
You're unique and sweet
I would still choose you if there were five of you.
I'm not trying to be spiteful. I rather just not pay to buy you.
I would rather give you what you want, to enlighten you.
But I won't take too much of your time out too.
I'm sorry but I felt like the light just shined right on you.
from the heavens,
I know it's just a quarter past 7
I'm already asking for your personal number so I can text it.
Listen I know life can get kind of hectic
there are better ways to make money than with sexing.
You don't have to sell all your goodies in the streets.
Miss I'm not trying to preach
just prying your eyes out of that sleep.
Just so you can see your fanny isn't cheap,
or shouldn't be a recipient of a receipt.
Butt, you're worth more than anything that you seek.
You cannot make yourself easily available to any freaking creep
That can pay for you or have his way with you,
for a million pennies.
Lady, I'm going to pray for you because I feel your empathy.
Sooner or later those open doors will be hard to close them.
temples should be sacred and only opened to the few chosen.
Because once you add a price to it,
it'll depreciate after its use.

I hope you act right and appreciate
this priceless advice that's abstruse
No, I'm not trying to down you
I just want to crown you.
Because I don't want them to find you, how I found you.
Miss I'm not here to save you, with a cape or a suit.
I hope these words help you change your ways of pursuit.
Butt, do what you want to do,
I'm not trying to clown you
I rather not treat you like a prostitute,
When I see that you are more honorable,
I won't judge you
but like the notorious glorious Ruth, I'll fight for you.
Hand for hand tooth for tooth, for the rights of you.
Just be safe and pray
no matter what decisions you choose to make
No matter what you do, never lose your faith.

LOST AND TURNED OUT

She belonged to the world. A lost little girl. Her thoughts went assail. She was lonely, tossed in a cell. Her beautiful body she would openly sell. I hope this goes well. If she could only cut off the tail and walk away from that shell. Find her way from the ever-winding trails. With pitchforks for her to derail. Confusions.... illusions.... intrusions entail. She's in the big city of Philly with liberty like a bell. She rings in promiscuity, and she won't say farewell. She doesn't discriminate against whom to date, whether it's males or females. She's been hurt way too much, but no one could tell because she hides it so well, behind a pretty smile. Meanwhile inside she's hurting like hell. She tries to not let the mistreatment be the reason that she fails or let the beatings stop her from achieving at Yale. Her family and friends don't care. She's like "oh well."

She's tired of living in despair and needs a new ship to sail. She knelt and asked God for forgiveness in a yell!

From giving in to a temptress while cyber surfing her Dell. She'll never reach the surface, to see her purpose prevail if she doesn't put her attention to the books on the shelf. She fell into the twilight-zone, lost the focus on herself. She was doing so good, and she could have excelled once she realized that she could just inhale, then exhale. Writing on the wall she couldn't read them with braille. She was so amazing, and her personality was contagious but got distracted and attracted to being rich and famous. Her goals got aimless. That's when she got lost in the sauce gainless from the madness then her thoughts became brainless. The detachments from the embarrassments of not having made her go backwards. She just had to have it.

She was a square from Delaware in the middle of Manhattan. When she got trapped in the lifestyle of fashions, madmen, and human trafficking. She was just an average chic and became a savage quick addictive lifestyle like an addict. Doing mad tricks, no magic. She caused havoc and appalled at everyone else's marriage. She didn't have the characteristics or the compassion. She couldn't make it; she kept clashing and crashing. Debilitating itches that she kept scratching by accident. She started bashing anyone who didn't have a gift to give to her, sabotaging her own wish that was sent to her. Lost in her thoughts amid a world that was fit for a girl to uplift from the abyss the twist and the twirls. It wasn't her fault. She paid the cost of the pimps and the pearls. Giving them control to sell her soul with an iron fist, she's a churl. Working the night shifts, her diamonds became her excitement. She got consignments from the ill-advised assignments. Until she got tested, molested, and arrested. Victimized by streets heading in the wrong direction. Her pool of thoughts was congested with alcohol and illicit medicines. Her illogical regimen only led to the devilish sediments. It wasn't until she hit rock bottom again when she got the message.

> She found love, she found God.
> She found self-attractiveness.
> She found peace, she found serenity
> She found self-happiness.
> She was no longer lost in her thoughts
> She found Jesus on the cross.
> She found passion again.
> She was saved.... Amen

Need help? United States:
1 (888) 373-7888
National Human Trafficking Hotline
SMS: 233733 (Text "HELP" or "INFO")
Hours: 24 hours, 7 days a week
Website: humantraffickinghotline.org

LET'S REVERSE THE CURSE

Here sis, grip my hand you're not alone. United we stand divided we fall to the pitfalls of the unknown. We need to stand tall and stick together against our common woes and foes. If we all get better at our problems, we'll be so powerful. We need to get out of the quicksand of the rich man's plans, withdrawals, and flip scams. Sis, get hipped to their flimflams. They got us going against each other just as God damned. We're supposed to be sisters and brothers and be there like fam. We shouldn't oppose or expose another on the instant gram, like the opps want us to do, which is in their plans. For instance, we will do better together if we ever get in a jam, but instead, we're resisting like them workout bands. Which is causing us to sever and that would never work out for us to advance, it would just lead to our severance. That's not the answer sis, we're going at each other's neck indirectly slandering. Can we have mutual respect so we can do some bandaging and manage to fix some of this injustice and corruption handling. Which to the US is so damaging. You ain't got to take out your phones or cross the street when you see me or start panicking, I come in peace. I may just want to greet, here's my hand again. Sheesh! I'm not your enemy, I just want to be your man friend, please, or someone who can help your needs if you need. But I understand your stance and respect your peace. You don't have to pretend to be uninterestingly uneasy just to get me to walk away, I get it I'm not a creep. You are overprotective but I respect it, maybe I should leave. You've been through a lot over these last 52 weeks. I can see your point of view. You got mad dudes trying to talk to you, being disrespectful and catcalling you. Grabbing on you being rude. So, let's move in a more positive direction. I don't want you to get confused or misconstrued by my message. I'm on your side. I may not know what you are going through, but I'll try to be more empathetic when I'm walking to you. I confess I may not be the best conversationalist, but my intentions are good. I was just being nice sis. I hope I'm not being misunderstood. But it seems like our enemy got us in a cold war too, that's awful. Got you in a defense mode when I'm just trying to talk to you. I'm just here to support you as your brother. I'm not going to force you to give in to my attempts to be cordial. I'll keep that door open. I am here for you whenever you need me. In the meantime, stay focused and you can say hi, if you see me. Until then, I'm praying we can end this Cold War that's going on between us. Because the truth is, we need y'all just as much as you need us.

MI$$ ME WITH THE BULLSPIT

Mi$$ me with the bullspit mi$$, I'm not a trick. Nor do I work hard at my job just to pay your bills and rent. We just met, can we chill a little bit. Can we have a sensational conversation that's intellectual, something that we can build with. Before we get sexual, I would like to let you know how I feel in a sense. I would like to get inside your mind and look right into your eyes and get really intense. After dating and relating, revealing our intents, we can have fascinating baecations over the hills and cliffs. Why are you looking at me funny talking about how you're hungry, are you really mi$$? Or do you just want me to spend all my money buying you meals and gifts? We never even kissed. How do you expect me to get you this as you persist? I don't get it; I'm not your critic but I find this quite ridiculous.

 Then you're asking me to light up big spliffs, then want to tell me you have a man when I want to grab your hand, I don't understand this mi$$. This is outlandish! How can I be your man if you already have one in your face. I rather not be your side piece that can be easily replaced. You shouldn't have even gotten in my car with no bra and silk lace seductively asking me for a ride when you're married if that was the case. Why would you want me to catch a case and get into a beef with a man that I didn't even know existed in the first place. You should've kept it brief instead of flirting and letting me skirt chase. You should be disgraced. How could you fix your face to ask me to pay for a bill that I didn't even help you create…. Ill.

Why would you approach me to suggest that I pay for a car note that you don't even want to pick me up for a date, oh no. You're doing the most thinking I would fall for the hoax with a convo that was faked…nope!!! Not for nothing I seen your game coming from a mile away, but I just kept a smile on my face because I was raised by women that were great. My auntie taught me how to be cordial and respectful in every way but it's becoming too costly to check for you queen when you're trying to checkmate me respectfully. They spoiled me royally, so why would I spend my hard-earned money on your jewelry and toiletries, for goodness' sake. Call me when you're free!!! Because I can't afford to keep paying attention to your greed, I have my own responsibilities.

You can mi$$ me with that bullspit baby, I was born gifted so there won't be any shopping sprees or trips to Macy's. No ifs ands or maybes, no you can't play me or try to get me to spend my valuable time chasing my desires or my di$K like Tracey. Maybe you're used to being with simps or lazy, or can it be that haze that got you a little hazy? Whatever it is that got you thinking that I'm about to spend my chips to

have sex with you and pay your fees, you must be special or crazy.
Mi$$ me with the bullspit, lady. I'm not trying to be mean or judgmental but I'm keen on principles. I'm just trying to let you know that I do value your mental and that your body is a temple. I wouldn't mind getting into your mind and treating you to nice things if you were mine. I just don't like sharing or being seasonal like some men do, I'm fine. So, I'll pass miss dash, but I'll get you that cab and we can split that tab in half like a Dutch. I'm a master at my craft. I just never been into paying to lay not trying to offend you in any way, but you can get paid in many other ways. I rather just have what money can't buy. I guess I'm just a different type of guy. Honestly, I respect your dishonesty, there's no need for an apology or my chime. But I'm more into being caring and sensual. So now since you know, mi$$

you can mi$$ me with the bullspit I'm not sweet like cinnamon rolls. I'm too valuable to spend my hard-earned dollars on you. I'm too blessed to be stressed going broke trying to buy a heart from you. So, halla at me boo when you ready to make a change until then I'm off ya. Yes, you're a dime but I shine like a quarter. This is just a penny for your thoughts, love. I have no problems courting ya, because you're a queen but I'm a King and this is what I was taught when I was brought up. I know the costs is up but I would rather feed your daughter than to get caught up in your web of deceit getting you to fly by the tarantula that you are.

Just mi$$ me with the bullspit and I say that emphatically with realness. You should have let me know from the rip your full intent, then give me the option before you ask me to take you shopping. My time, my mind or my money isn't an object I intend to waste on nonsense. So be honest, then we can get beyond this. Being broke is just a spirit that we inherit when we don't pay attention to the realest gift and that's the present. So, if you need it and I got it I will help you. I just can't afford your tricks of erotic psychosis just to clothe and shelter you. I can show you better than I can tell you save them trix, mi$$ serial gold digger sugar baby. Be a lady then maybe I can buy you fine jewels and wine and dine you, just not on day two. I just met you. Let me respect you before you ask me to spend a check on you. Have some class and dignity before you ask me to trick my cheese. If you really wanted to get with me, we could've gone to Mickey D's or Applebee's and got to really know each other more accurately. So, mi$$ me with the bullspit baby and pass that weed.

IT WAS HER

We come from the same mother. So, I have no other choice but to love ya. Just for the simple fact of you being my brother I have the utmost respect for ya. But, why do you have to treat her like you don't need her? That's messed up and not acceptable. She was your first leader.

It was her.... Who fed you your first vegetable? Who treated you as if you were special. Who never ever left you or neglected you.

It was her.... Who kept you. Who breast fed you. Who bred you. Who inserted you into her busy hectic schedule.
It was her.... The one who raised you. Who made you brother? Who kept you away from the gutters. Who'd made sure that you were tougher?

It was her.... Who loved you when you didn't even know what love was. It was your dad that gave her them drugs, but to him you hold no grudge.

It was her.... Who shielded you from them cold streets? When the police gave us no peace or relief, kid. Where's the love bruh? She needs it! Don't be so impetuous.

It was her.... She was the one, who tucked you under them comforters, when they wanted to come for us. You only get one mother.... brother!!! Button up!

It was her.... Who spread the toast with the butter? Who protected us with the toast when the busters wanted to confront us, what's up with ya?

It was her.... Who changed the sheets when you used to pee and wet the bed now you got a big head, and you don't want to give her no bread? It's a cold world. It was her, not ole girl that cared for you and was there for you before your toes could even curl. Now she can't even get an answer at all when she calls what if she's sick. Not even on Christmas?

It was her.... Who even gave you your first gift, and that was life!!! Now it's like, she's out of sight out of mind. she gave you those nice eyes, are you blind? You can't even find a little bit of time to spend, and that's priceless. It seems like you spend more time on your devices and on your right wrist.

It was her.... Who gave you your first advice to get rich? Who sacrifices her sins to invite you in? That isn't righteous, or right kid. At night she just sits... and think about the life that she had to give up to give to you. You don't have to ridicule. That's not nice sis. We all have our wrongs that we got to go through. But can we all get along and be strong like a family's supposed to do? Even though she was drugged up, she made sure there was food on them tables and Kool-Aid in them cups, bruh. So how can you just ignore her, if it wasn't for her, you wouldn't have such and such or the ability to succeed. Yeah, this sucks that much, it's killing me.

It was her.... Who made sure we had cable and Nintendo's. She made you, so why are you throwing shades and innuendoes.

It was her.... Who kept the cold from coming in them dark rainy windows, but you ghosted her face when things couldn't be all so simple.

It was her.... Who gave you something to eat, stuffing them turkeys on every Thanksgiving. Who gave you strength when you were weak, you should thank her for living!!! You should give grace and show your face to that woman and appreciate all that she has given. Why do you have so much hate and resentment?

It was her.... Who made sure she got to them appointments to get them food stamps and ointments. No need to be rude champ life is good, you should enjoy it.

It was her.... Who sheltered us in them shelters when things went helter-skelter. When no other men would help us, not even unemployment. They only wanted to be her toy-friend, for their enjoyment, but you were just her little boy then. She sold her body and soul for you not to go in that hole, of a system that corrupted us and led me to parole and prison. Just in case you're forgetting... Yeah us, your other siblings. Wow, now you're acting all swollen and indifferent. Not even Michael Jordan would've had a championship without Scottie Pippen. That's a fact, so stop tripping and being malignant.

It was her.... Who matured you from the beginning, who adored you and gave you toys as an infant. Who instilled hustling in the core of you, for you to get it.

It was her.... Who spent chips on your first gift, be wise and sincere. She gave you your life, the air, the chance to be a millionaire. That's not polite or fair. She gave you your feet and hands to fight. Ears to listen, stop acting trifling, she shouldn't have to ask you twice when you're tripping. Because you wouldn't be here if she didn't make that ultimate sacrifice ya hear? How can you just leave her there in despair, then disappear, that's weird.

It was her.... Who cared, who spared, and who carried you for nine months. That is nothing that can be compared. Come here, put aside them blunts and man up. You got it twisted and your vision is impaired. For her you should stand up, not sit in that chair. She could have aborted you or not afforded you, but she chose to hold you, mold you and show support for you.

It was her.... She was there, she flaunted you and taught you. Who you thought brought you to every function at school?

It was her… That's who!!! She put aside her potential fortunes for you. How come she's not that important to you? What's wrong with you? She may not have been the best at buying. But at least I can attest and testify to it, that she made the best of our environment. Nevertheless, she could never rest her eyelids. She was going through so much emotional distress smoking cigarettes just to relieve her stress. She could have given you away to adoption while you wept. But she didn't choose that option, to neglect or pass you like a test. But, yet she had so many problems back then. She slept with many men just trying to make a dollar out of fifty cents. She was your hustler, not from Hollis, but your queen from Yonkers. So acknowledge her then pay homage. While she was out there copping, choosing bad options, she chose to not have you sent away or locked in the system. It was her, not them!!! Who moved you out of the hoods of Yonkers, where it was so rough and violent, I don't know if you would've survived it, you should apologize quick!!!

It was her.... Who gave us M&Ms to stop our stomachs from grumbling. Maybe she got high because her mind was tumbling and fumbling, or she couldn't find enough help to keep her from stumbling. Doing it all by herself with nothing to grip her feet to keep from plummeting. As a single parent with just minimal assistance from the government. You were too young to understand it then. The love she would give.

It was her.... Who took turns in the wrong direction looking for protection and a safe haven for you to rest your head in. You was a chance that she took but never regretted. You was the man in her book, her substantial investment. She could've never forgotten you.

It was her.... Who gave up her cookies and juices just so you can have an empire, I am not lying like luscious, she rode the road of life with thin tires. We may not have grown up like the Huxtables, but she had love for you and made sure that your crib was comfortable.

It was her.... Who stayed up and prayed for you to make a way for you. Now she can't get back the interest from the attention that she paid to you.

It was her.... Who gave you your first car. Even though it was a hot wheel you drove far. She instilled you to be driven with ambition to go hard. She put you in the position to win and be your own star. To rise like the yeast in them cakes she use to bake for you on your birthdays.

It was her.... that gave you your first day in the first place. So, appreciate her while she's living because at any instance she can be taken away?

Chapter 2: Hope

ART OF WAR

The greatest trick the devil ever played was to make you think that God never existed. He doesn't want you to prevail he'll rather see you in hell or sleeping with the fishes or swimming in a well... wishing. Well, this tale is different. As you can see these racial injustices are starting to happen more frequent and indecent. They're still Willie Lynching, but now they're just conveniently remixing it. The slave slaughterhouse is the new police precinct. So, bro, before you go thinking about taking another brother's life. Blink twice, then give him a pass just for the sake of another life. Please, make that sacrifice for the passion of Christ, we're all brothers from another mother that should be suffice. We're made in God's images, so don't fall for the gimmicks and the tricknology. They brutalized our men and women. We weren't even offered retribution or apologies. The real enemies are the law makers and their racist formalities and the crooked government who oppress us with their technology. They made it hard for US to get properties and doctorate degrees. Only through these analogies, that I can profess then manifest my knowledge tree. I hope y'all can start to see the apollo's creed, through my artfully whole heartily poetry. Check out my IG and follow me socially. Kings killing kings isn't the way it's supposed to be. For us to succeed we must not let envy or greed grow in these streets. We must peacefully equally see that our needs are met expediently. Then immediately kept by sentries for centuries. Knowledge can set you free mentally. Take a seat and see you'll be intrigued eventually. Inshallah, if it was meant to be, it will be. If it's in His creed, then no one can mislead the will of His Deen. Hopefully you'll take heed, and something can grow from these holy mustard seeds that was sown for you to reap. Trust in His decree. Never get it confused we were used and abused by them creeps.

Our 40 acres and a mule are being gentrified right now as we speak. By the same fascist racists that instilled genocide and homicides à la mystique. It's deep, but it's also connected to them dollar signs that we often seek. All the money we're making is evaporating like a moral disease. Expending on vacations and expensive rides and toiletries. Plus, the tax you are paying is employing them chauvinistic luxuries, but you're too stuck to see because your eyes are glued to a smart tv which isn't smart to me. They have cameras on them dots identifying US by our faces breaching our privacies. C the opps rather keep us chained or boxed, fenced like the oddest odyssey obviously. Luckily there's nothing that these thieves can do to stop God's prophecy for US to succeed, but you got to believe. They'll rather keep US in suspense with our souls naked, that's only the tip of the iceberg. They're cold like the tolls they be taking. Our Job opportunities are vacant all going overseas to Asians, I hope you see through the mayhem, they ain't playing. The locks we got to break them. We're gonna make it, even if we got to take it to see the beauty in this filthy Amerikkkan Pegan pageants. They will steal our legacies and recipes and then our credits they'll erase it and replace it, bro I can't let this be. They created statutes with face lifts. Even if I tried, I couldn't make this up. This is way past foul it's flagrant and fake as ugh. But this technique is ancient, Sun Tzu taught this in 556 B.C. before Christ was attempted to be tempted by Satan. So have patience be cool if you were paying attention in school, we're all immigrated Egyptians. America history is tainted, now they don't even want US to mention this. The hieroglyphics are amazing. their saying I'm a Muslim Protestant Christian or whatever you want to make of it. I'm just a prodigal son that was missing, that came back home glistening, because of what them lifer OGs said I was listening.
Life is provisioning. I'm just envisioning it....

Quantum Leaps

Just to let you know, I would never forget or quit. Those words in my vocabulary do not exist. Even though you may have slipped, God would never let you fall into an abyss or a bottomless pit. I know what it feels like to grow up fatherless, kid. I was still able to achieve honorable accomplishments. The roads may have had mad ditches, distractions, and glitches. But to Allah's astonishment I was still able to find a way because I listened when I heard His admonishments and then repented. After giving him my admissions, our relationship became immaculate. So, whether you're a Muslim, Christian or a Catholic, it's all about your submission to him, and that's it… period. I find that to be quite accurate, but my problems weren't easily fixed. I was wrapped in sins. Then I got sent to the department of corrections. Which was like a college for misfits. They were just teaching me how to recidivate back to their desks and receptionist. To which I culminately became more reckless to be honest. They were more concerned with collecting a check. No disrespect your Honor miss, but all they gave me was cards with missing kings in them decks, a wretched etch a sketch, and puzzles that had different pieces from what I can recollect. I had to get consequential attention just to get recognition. In retrospect I was multiplying the division. I was alive but I wasn't living. My mathematicians were incorrect, and that led me to misconstrue their solutions. Which in turn left me with more confusion and my medulla with mucus and contusions. I was in school, but I never followed rules then. I got beat by rulers in detention for not paying attention. My childhood wasn't good; my parents weren't too attentive.

Drugs were getting abused while I was getting used by older women. The thugs I viewed that I thought were cool, are all doing lengthy prison sentences. I was also used as a punching bag by a drugged-up stepdad that stepped on my hand every chance that he had. My lunch was a bag filled with leftovers from leftovers. Every crumb that he had went to his blunt or his flask when he slept over. He never left sober. I turned to the streets who accepted me like a wrecked soldier. Which in return had me seek different parents apparently, I was messed over. That's when I met Jehovah, and witnessed for the first time that I can turn over the sins of my flesh and have a fresh do-over. If it wasn't for the prayers, I wouldn't be here!!! God isn't a mystery he's within me let's be clear. I survived only by His grace to let you know that he isn't fake. You don't have to let your mistakes be a narrative of your fate. If you fell 7 times, get up and make the 8th great. Prayer plus work equals faith. Make it work and work it straight, it's worth its weight. It is never too late to make a change. You can start now why wait. Don't let this precious time escape.

NEVER EVER QUIT

Thy shall never ever quit!
Stay awake and educated
You can make it through this
You're great never speculate it

Yes, your good enough for whatever
There's nothing that you can't conquer
Keep it up you're only going to get better
Only YOU can stop the way for you to prosper

Even when the skies are grey
The sun will eventually shine one day
Hardships are only temporary
God's strengths are forever and sturdy

Failure is just an experience for success
Sometimes to find the right answers to a test
When things get tough hold on to your faith
You made it this far mine's well finish the race
Trust your gut it will never lie to your face

You wouldn't be in a situation
If you don't have what it takes
Sometimes God will put you in a tough space
Just so you can remember his grace.
You may not know why,
but keep striving it's all fate.
You already have the tools to survive

in whatever may come your way.
Quitting is not an option.
Giving up isn't the answer.
With self-belief and the lord
You can be confident.
You can overcome anything,
Even cancer and coronavirus.

American Cancer Society,
Cancer information, answers, and hope.
Available every minute of every day.
1-800-227-2345

HOPE

I can't even imagine how you must feel
All I can do is empathize
I know the pain can be so real
When a loved one is sent to the sky
We will never know why
Because it's all in God's plans
Beyond what we can see with the naked eye
Sometimes it may be hard for us to understand
Lady, its okay to cry here's my hand.
Hold your head up high, fist in the air.
It seems like we're living in a time

Where people just don't t care
it can be so hard to get by
when it seems worse than it appears
Especially when you don't know why
and it seems to be unfair

But when you trust in God.
He goes against all the odds
Even when your fallen hard
you can always call on God

He will always be there every time
Your prayers are never declined
Heavens gates has opened wide
To accept your child's immortal soul
They was chosen from the most high
So stay focused and never let go

I hope you remain strong it's going to be okay
I hope you turn that frown into a smile
I hope that you have a wonderful day
I hope you know that he's safe in heaven now
Watching down over you and protecting you
As your very own special guardian angel
your child was very exceptional
Now he can live through you while blessing you
Hold on....

Even though they're gone
They're here with you
They will never be forgotten
As their legacy continues
like the sun in the sky
They will forever shine
Never stop the grind
Maintain a positive mind
All we can do is take it one day at time
One step at a time in this journey called life
I know the feeling is tough
And you can't let it go
I know the pain can become rough
And unbearable
Have faith better days is soon to be coming
There's nothing wrong with bearing your soul
Let it all out, I'm here I'm not running
Besides I care, I hope you know
there are things in life that cannot be controlled
now his spirits are with you everywhere you go
I hope you know God, and have faith
Their life wasn't lived in vain
but now they are in a better place
Away from the suffering away from the pain
I hope you smile at their pictures
When you look at their face
And feel proud when you consider
That they're in a much better place
with honor and dignity here is a rose

Life is precious, and time is perpetual
Just to let you know
Everything happens for a reason
even when you can't see it
Never ever stop believing
I feel your passion and I feel your grieves.
Having faith is believing what you cannot see
Not everything will make sense to you and me
But trust in God and you will succeed.
The word of God says vividly and clearly:
"Lean not to your own understanding
And trust in he."

Continue to have hope and faith
Justice will prevail eventually.

> THERE ARE PEOPLE WHO CARE AND CAN HELP.
> **YOU ARE NOT ALONE.**
>
> **CRISIS TEXT LINE:**
> TEXT **HOME** TO 741741
>
> **NATIONAL SUICIDE PREVENTION LIFELINE**
> CALL 1-800-273-TALK (8255)
>
> EMERGENCY? SEEK HELP - **CALL 911**
>
> **SMS: 988**
> **call.**

DON'T DO IT!

Nooooo!!!!
don't do it!!!!
No suicide.
At times I didn't want to be here either
But I would rather for you to do than die
We all have been scrutinize
sometimes it can be hard when you're mis-utilized
to separate truths from lies
but between you and I
we can find a solution
We all go through it
Life can be stressful

. Hold on
there's no telling what the future lies
Besides.... You're not alone
We all have our woes and worries
though your circumstances may look blurry
This too shall pass. He's in control. God is sturdy
You're too precious to be giving your life away
Your future will see more brighter days
If it's in God's will then he will find a way
Can I invite you to pray?
I was also scared of living
and didn't see the intentions that God had for me
I felt like no one was there when I got sentenced
and they all just laughed at me
But I'm glad to see, that I made the right decision
not to end my life in that prison
That would've been a tragedy, a crash collision
Even though I felt like the justice system
was corrupted and after me
being vindictive, all about a buck harassing me
but somehow I made it through to talk to you
Please don't give up I will walk with you
Take this path with me
Don't do it!!!
It may seem dark
but there's light at the end of the tunnel
I know this, I understand your grieves
and feelings of hopelessness
but think about all the people that love you
They would be devastated if you go through this
Refocus.
Don't do it!!!

If I would've listened to the whispers in the air
I wouldn't be here
I'm no different than you, sitting in those chairs
I'm just like you, I got problems too but I care
It's hard to see things when your mind isn't clear
Especially when you're stressing, it gets weird
That could turn into depression and fears
I did nine years in prison
For a crime I never committed
I was left there with no remissions
So, I know how it feels to be neglected disrespected
And treated reckless by your peers
But forget them
I know how it feels when nobody cares
But you have to hold on
Stay strong and persevere
I have personally been there
So I can tell you from my past life experience.
Life isn't fair.
Don't do it!!!
I too wanted to give up and quit
But I didn't do it, so I get it
I'm not trying to be your critic or judge you
As a matter of fact, I think that you're terrific
And God loves you.
You are gifted
There's a purpose for you
Your life is worth living
There is another version of you

So don't let a temporary emotion affect you
To make a permanent decision
Trust me, it's really worth it to be living
Because you can turn that current infliction
Into a positive outcome successful reviction
You're blessed just by the simple fact of you waking
Up this morning somebody else didn't
Please listen!!!
Don't do it!!!
Please think it through
Your family loves and need you
Without you they would be miserable
Please be Considerable
Don't do it!!!

THERE ARE PEOPLE WHO CARE AND CAN HELP
YOU ARE NOT ALONE.
CRISIS TEXT LINE:
TEXT HOME TO 741741
NATIONAL SUICIDE
PREVENTION LIFELINE
CALL 1-800-273-TALK (8255)
EMERGENCY? SEEK HELP - CALL 911

988 Suicide and Crisis Lifeline
Hours: Available 24 hours. Languages: English, Spanish

NO HOPE IN DOPE

Nooooo!! I don't want you to have an overdose.
I hope that you cope, there's no hope in dope.
Nope, bro don't you fall for the okey doke.
Noooo! Don't do it! Please, slow your role.
Life is too beautiful for you to just lose it.
Whatever you're going through, you have to go through it.
Don't be foolish, life is filled with cruel illusions.
I want you to enjoy these truth fruitful fusions.
Take your mind off your stresses and the confusions.
I know, you're going through a lot you ain't got to prove it.
The truth is hard to deal with when you're going thru it.
Reality can get sick, but there's room for improvement.

I know how it feels when no one seems to understand you,
and it seems like life always have the upper hand on you.
When doors are crashing through, and you can't seem to handle
and it's one thing after another dammn... Daniel!!! Sun

don't live your life in vain or let it go down the drain.
Those drugs in your hand will only make things worse again.
I know it feels at first like it takes away all your hurts and pains.
But it will only temporarily relieve, not reverse the curse in your veins.
Things will go berserk and get in the way of your work.
It'll have mama praying at church giving change out her purse.
Hoping you change your strange ways before your bubble burst.
You said the last time was the last time because it doesn't work.

You just got too many problems churning fast in your mind.
It feels like you can't focus to get past the past for your grind.
You are hoping that this potion takes away all your problems.
You can't seem to solve them. They just keep revolving.
If it does it's only for a moment, it's a false temporary feeling.

Nope don't do it!!!
Problems would just get harder and the karma will start building.
Feelings of hopelessness for your loved ones isn't appealing.

Nooo Don't do it!!!
For the sake of your parents and your children. I hope you understand
to them your worth more than millions
How do you think they'll feel at your wake, wake up!
I know what you're dealing with... wait!!! Uhhhh!!!
It's when you become sick and tired of being sick and tired.
That you want to quit and give up those desires,
but you don't realize it. That's when you'll decide to quit
and kick those nasty bad habits and admit you're an addict.
Don't wait until it's too late!!!
When you're feeling like a silly wabbit in that casket.
Looking up at them, like why??? I just had to have it.
But it's okay you're not alone with God by your side.
You don't have to do this on your own, you know why?
He feels your passion. You don't have to cry.

You just have to ask him.
It's like the law of attraction but only that it's backwards.
You can reverse the curse. There's no satisfaction in an addict.
At first it hurts but whatever you lose you can get it back quick.
The 12 steps to recovery will become automatic with practice.
But first you must admit to yourself that you are an addict,

and that your addiction is out of control and unmanageable.
You must believe a greater power than you can handle your soul.
Such as He, the almighty G.O.D. That can restore you back to sanity,
you just have to understand it thoroughly with clarity.
Give all your problems to him and work with the faculties.
Then make a clear decision to give God the permission
to guide you through the mission, to be normal again.
Your sobriety you have to defend it when D-rugs calls you again,
because he will be relentless, but you must ignore it my friend.

Then it's mandatory that you take a good look in the mirror
and make a moral inventory so that you can see things clearer.
Then get rid of your active using friends that's causing hysteria.
No guts no glory, you got to lose the fear and butts.
Once you admit to yourself,
you can share and compare to others that's in similar situations
it won't seem weird.

Your real peers will be there to support and cheer you up.
You must be willing to let God do his job, keep in touch.
Because insanity ends when responsibility begins.
Then you'll ready to make amends to your family and friends,
That you crossed and lost when you were off in insanity sauce.
Hopefully, inshallah they will show some remorse.
Then of course you'll have to continue to take self-reflection.
One day at a time, taking reps, heading in the right direction.
Things will get better as these steps you start to climb.
Leave all the toxic people, places, and things all behind.

With prayer you will start to see improvements in increments.
With faith and persistence, you will get through this.
You are not alone with God, you can do this.

He's the king of the throne and pronounced victory over this.
Like Nike, Apollo Creed, and Sly Stone. Once that spirit awakens, you will start to re-see your greatness.
That comes from practice, you must replace the bad habits.
It's one day at a time, have patience.
It's one step at a time, you can make it.
Don't forget to pray to him. Amen.
Stay on your grind!!!

SAMHSA Related Inquiries
Find Help and Treatment
The National Helpline provides 24-hour free and confidential referrals and information about mental and/or substance use disorders, prevention, treatment, and recovery in English and Spanish.

<u>SAMHSA's National Helpline</u>
<u>800-662-HELP (4357)</u>
TTY: <u>800-487-4889</u>

UNITY IN MY COMMUNITY

What I want?.... Is peace and unity in this universe. But It's going to take you and me to do it first. Whether you go to a church or go to the mosque. We got to put God first, and trust in the almighty Allah. What counts is praying to God and your submission. To me a religion is just another form of control and/or a division. I love you for the sake of Allah no matter what your religion is. Whether you're Catholic, Muslim, or Christian, it's your business. My passion and my mission is serving God with conviction. If we stick together, we can fight and win this racist system. But it's going to take him, me, you, her, and them to win this. We would have to all come together forever to end this.

Let's put aside our differences and unite to fight for a cause. Separation only keeps the US limited; we can right all our wrongs. I'm not a racist, I've been victimized by the system since I was 5. I was put in situations where I was meant to die. But by the grace of the forever forgiving God, I'm still alive. I was embraced when I had to face the odds but still, I survived. In my testament I was tested and arrested by them. Indigested in prison that was congested with men and destined to be condemned by their strict negative regimens. They were prejudiced because of the resilience of my skin. Predators of my kin, despiteous of the coronation within. Every day I wake up another black man's soul is being taken up. By cops with barbaric behaviors trying to tame us with their guns and lethal tasers aimed at us. We're targeted by the same ones who claim they're afraid of us. They were sworn to defend us but betrayed us by maiming us. They're trying to end us in more ways than one whether it's by the gavel or the gun, plus they're after our funds. We must not $upport them, buying their clothes and jewelry. Let's start businesses, then reinvest in our own communities. They want you and me to drink liquor and smoke weed. Then how can we be the best we can be, choking our dreams. If we're unfocused mentally. This should alarm US. It's no joke we need unity;, they're using felonies to disarm US. This isn't how it's supposed to be, we are Kings and Queens not niggers, prisoners, crackheads, or dope fiends. If there's no justice, then it will definitely be no peace. We must not sleep until we see the change that we seek. In God we trust, but the works got to come from US, you and me.

Dear Amerikkka

Dear Amerikkka...
Why are you so scared of us? We went from the back of the bus, to owning houses and trucks. We built this country up, now you want our mouths to be shut. You tried to hush us up with a stimulus, but that amount wasn't enough it was ridiculous.

Dear Amerikkka...
Why do you keep locking us up in prisons?
Is it to separate us from our children and women?
To leave them without strength and wisdom to make decisions? Or is it to nullify our reproductive system? Is that why microwaves are positioned at our crotches in prison? Is that why our food is filled with saccharine, estrogen mixes which causes Alzheimer's and dementia dimensions?

Dear Amerikkka...
Why do you like to incite us to kill each other in the prisons. Leaving US stressed, depressed, hopeless and wishing. Having no other outlets but violence, mail, and visits. Stabbing each other so you don't have to do it is vicious.

Dear Amerikkka...
Why do you counter our peaceful protest conjunctions? Against the police brutality and injustices? Is it because you support inequality and the judicial corruption? Or is it to protect your racist presidents to function, because their enabling y'all to still get rich as we're tumbling?

Dear Amerikkka...
We're still feeling the aftermath of the willie lynching. You incited a war between US black men and women. Leaving

us with no insight causing hell in our kitchens there's no love or trust. We're going against each other just like you wanted us. You predicted this with your wicked premonitions. Why do you still want to enslave us what is your intentions?

Dear Amerikkka...
Why do you want to deprive us of healthcare then give us unfair treatment and mistreat us at the hospitals? Why do you want to keep us on welfare and not teach us to gain and retain our own capital? Why that is there's fast-food and liquor stores on every corner in the ghetto? Is it to poison us, so we can be unhealthy and illogical? Or is it to flood our cities with drugs to entrap our opportunities to make our success almost impossible? I know you don't want to see our communities with no type of unity. But it's so unfortunately to see that you love to make your fortunes from us in sports proceeds and raise the cost for us to breathe. Shall I proceed? We're not welcome in your gated societies, so why do you want to live and gentrify in our poverty properties?

Dear Amerikkka...
We're not scared of ya, as a matter of fact we're prepared for ya. We're sick of tired of your oppression. We're not going to let you do what you did to our ancestors we're not forgetting or regressing. We're not going to let you take us back to slavery, the Great Depression or the '08 recession. It's time for us to stand up and give you a taste of your own medicine.

COLD KNIGHTS

Instead of you telling me
I rather for you to provide it for me
then maybe I would accept your non apology
I know that you're probably tired of me
but honestly, I'm going to try to keep it brief
for reasons that's obvious, see...
I already know you won't allow me to achieve
with your foot on my neck, I can't swallow or breathe
but the almighty Allah empowers me to succeed

So, I'll share my favorite methodology, Hadith...
"WHEN YOU SEE A PERSON WHO HAS BEEN GIVEN MORE THAN YOU IN MONEY AND BEAUTY, THEN LOOK TO THOSE WHO HAVE BEEN GIVEN LESS"

That truthfully suits me I'm blessed
Then I humbly ask Allah for peace within me
and to accept my apologies
Hopefully he can help me control my stress and anxiety.
I'm never the one who is filled with envy or jealousy
but I do sometimes wonder how this can be
that I'm compelled to poverty.
While I keep my Integrity
and my hustler's ambition proprietary
as my mission linchpin and proceed nonviolently
I was raised in a capitalist society
that told me to go get my own salary,
the cost of living is getting higher than these calories.
I rather get a job than to rob
I never looked at the next man's cheese
I accept my own improv poverty reality
I rather work than scam for checks I'm a King
I have respect and principalities
I'm going to stretch my hands
and invest my grands properly
And not blow it like the wretched sands of the Mojave
Then possibly
I hope that all my good intentions Allah sees
and I'm forgiven for my sins
like I have forgiven my enemies

P.E.A.C.E.

WILL YOU

This is a bad time to do a crime
Think twice and be nice
It's better to live another day
Get the hell out of the Devil's way
This time will pass, get pass the past
Just use the same faith, that you already have
You got to have patience or end up as a patient
Because the devil will be waiting
waiting and waiting!!!
Take it one day at a time, one step at a time
Never let the day take too much of your mind.
Pray prey and pray, for a better day
Don't let them take your peaceful serenity away
Stay positive and hold on to your faith
God got this, where there's a will there's a way

2+2=4

My time's 2 precious

2 be wasted on guessing

Please don't ever 4get it. —CGM

Flaws and disorders

It's crazy how they just torched and tortured him. Just because of the thoughts of the color of his skin. I'm amazed how they keep abusing their powers this happens so often. These cowards didn't even show any remorse for him; His life was forced to end. I have seen and been through this countless times in this awful wrench. Thank God that I survived, and I was one of the some that was more fortunate. These are the types of actions that actually happen often in the hood. Factually, I have never met a cop that was good. Back then the deaths weren't reported because it didn't get recorded. I've seen so many black youth's lives get distorted. I have seen so many kids get robbed by cops of their future or a big portion of it. All because of a corrupted Judge, or a lawyer that couldn't be afforded. All of this is unfortunately incautious, fruits from slavery and the Willie Lynch courses. It's all true you can see the proof in the flaws of the laws that they are endorsing, they've been unremorsefully enormously mis-enforcing. But a change is not going to happen just by voicing our choices. We have to actively be proactive, sadly we must force them. Of course, in nonviolent ways our acts must be thoughtful and brave. We have to fight fire with water. I'm tired of taking losses. For example, you can start with not supporting them. Whether it's by votes or revolt we got to do our portion or end up in a coffin or back in a modern-day slavery metamorphosis or be lost in the matrix reality, asleep like Morpheus.

Wake up!!! Wake up from this awfulness

PREY 4 FREEDOME

*Please give me **Freedome** in my mind lord.*
When I feel locked up and down and out.

*Please give me **Freedome** in my mind lord.*
When I'm caged in by loneliness and doubts.

*Please give me **Freedome** in my mind lord.*
When I feel imprisoned by my past decisions.

*Please give me **Freedome** in my mind lord.* When my anxiety is getting the best of me and I don't feel like living.

*Please give me **Freedome** in my mind lord.*
When I'm boxed in by my fears and guilty consciousness.

*Please give me **Freedome** in my mind lord.*
When I'm feeling overwhelmingly weak and acting obnoxious.

*Please give me **Freedome** in my mind lord.*
When I'm confused, feeling used and abused and I'm about to tweak.

*Please give me **Freedome** in my mind lord.*
So I can accept your words, and your blessing and your lessons every day of the week.

*Please give me **Freedome** in my mind lord.*
So I can feel your peace and love, and be able to love again.

*Please give me **Freedome** in my mind lord.*
So I can keep my head above these waters and know the difference between my enemies and my friends.

*Please give me **Freedome** in my mind lord.*
So I can bond with others that you send to my life to help me get right with my family .

*Please give me **Freedome** in my mind lord.*
So I can sleep in peace while I'm alive. Hopefully you can help me get back my sanity.

*Please give me **Freedome** in my mind lord.*
So that I can be the person you created me to be and give ye the glory.

*Please give me **Freedome** in my mind lord.*
So that I can praise you and pray to you faithfully and thank you for not ignoring me.

*Please give me **Freedome** in my mind lord.*
So I can be the best I can be and have my cypher complete so I can teach the seeds.

*Please give me **Freedome** in my mind lord.*
So I can let go of D-evils that's haunting me. Please mentally set me free.

REVOLUTION SOLUTION

I used to grind in the midst just to shine like I'm rich, but the game was designed to keep my mind in a twist. Not to resign and climb up out of it and resist. So, I could subconsciously submit to have my talents just stripped, right out of my prime. Got kicked out of my mom's and those psalms just slipped, right out of my palms. With cuffs on my wrist, I fell asleep in the abyss. At least I admit that I was wrong a little bit. I was weak I repent. I didn't mean to cause no harm.

I was sick. I was addicted to getting unprosperous chips. I was trapped in the street hustler's bottomless pit. In fact, I didn't adjust to becoming a fatherless kid. But Inshallah I would weather this storm, so I could forever live long, my words are my bond. Yeah, the trap was a trick because those crackers would just sit….. Back in recline and let those packages flip. So, they could enslave us without cracking their whips. Then come back to where we live and start attacking us in our cribs. They would shoot us and tase us, to detach us from our kids. Then unlawfully detain us giving us irrational bids. They would intrude us and degrade us and until we loot up their neighborhood, they'll never get the message, if all we do is pray for good. They would never respect us until they feel our pain. All this peaceful protesting and we still haven't seen a change. It is so outrageous, that being black is dangerous. They don't want us to raise up to be presidents or Lakers. We had to dodge the draft to become champs and medalists. Our genetics are greater, we're more advanced than medicines. While they design generics, copy, and paste our rhetoric. Our biometrics and heritage are divinely inherited. All that systematic inequality equals passive oppression. We must revolt not vote, because they rigged the last election.

Chapter 3: Pain Chronicles

PAINGRY

I'm so tired of waking up feeling paingry. I swear to God that only God can understand me. How irritable and emotional I can be. It feels like this pain is taking hold of me. It has me spazzing out uncontrollably. Like I wish that God would just take this toll off me. I've been clean for a year somehow, so now, I'm doing all this soberly. Because I know that parole would smoke me like potpourri. You may think that it's all good now like how it's supposed to be when you see my million-dollar smile. Like wow, when you're approaching me. Or my shades that I may hide behind brokenly because I don't want you or anyone else to notice me. Usually, I don't wear my feelings emotionally on my sleeves, but this pain is so deep that I could barely go to sleep. When I dial up my friends all I hear is beeps.... Then answering machines. They don't answer when they know it's me. Because they think that I am going to ask them for help ferociously. So, I guess I'll do this all by myself, anti-socially. This got me so paingry! God, please help me. *Can someone please pray for me?* I feel so helplessly. My friends don't understand my grief. They be laughing and joking, I'm unfocused and I can barely breathe. *Can you please pray for me?* I can't seem to keep a girl or a friend because I'm depressed, bitter and in distress I need a cigarette. Yes, this gets me so vexed and stressed. I'm trying my best but I'm starting to feel hopeless. Sometimes I wish my oppressors would just slit my throat and wrist, because I don't have the courage or the strength to go through it. Sometimes I wish I would get thrown in a ditch. But I need to get up out of this mess I'm in. I'm hurting!!! My body is still pounding, this Percocet is worthless. All it gave me was an itch and a false temporary sense of relief. It only built up a tolerance and unfortunateness, my losses just peaked. My unawareness of the surroundings I'm lost in, so is my physique. I don't watch what I eat or floss my teeth. My attitude stinks. You could smell it through my speech. Pessimistic negativity attracts negativity just leave me be. These cheap Aleve's never cured my headaches. I don't know where my life is heading, I'm weak. I'm unbalanced, it feels like I'm drowning in my sleep. I'm so sick and tired of being sick and tired on repeat. Laying in this bed again, waking up to generic medicines. I need something more potent than these ibuprofens and Excedrin's. I have been going through the motion's brethren. I'm unfocused. My problems are repetitive. As they all say that I should just relax and pray, but I feel so miserable and pitiful I've been napping all day. I'm going to try to adjust and hold my faith, bow my head and pray and let God lead the way. *Please pray for me*. I need it today. All I can say is thanks R.I.P. to Hank, he was braver and a brewer. Sometimes I just wanna hug my mom's you would too if you knew her. *Please pray for me*. I need to get my thoughts out of the sewer. I tried to do good butt my maneuvers got me in deep manure. There's nothing else you could say to me. *Please pray for me*. Maybe God will make a way for me. I'll just wait and see patiently. While I'm paingry crying like a big baby, this pain is making me angry. With no one or nothing by my side to help me pacify. I don't know whether I want to laugh, cry or die. Then I'll think about what would happen if I tried and succeeded. Then I'd think about my family, how much they love me, and I'm needed. Then I think about Jesus, how he died for my sins. So, I'll call on him because I'm in dire need of Him.

Please pray for me Please pray for me pray for me please.

I'M PAINGRY TOO!!!

I'm sick and tired of being sick and tired, everybody's lying and not even trying to hide it. Everyone I grew up with is either dead, in toxic relationships or in the feds striving and surviving. I'm tired of people's pessimism, it's such a nuisance. If I added up their two cents, I would've been rich! I think the higher that I get the lower that it takes me, then I start to slip into emotionlessness and get paingry! I'm tired of wasting my time and energy. I don't know what I'm buying. I'm tired of my doctors mistreating me as if I'm his drug client as he implies it. My chiropractor just cracks my back then hands me a paper to sign it. This girl keeps coming over, not sober, her phone is on silent. I'm tired of being paingry, I'm constantly in pain and I'm angry. Even my own family calls me a tyrant strangely. My preacher's teachings I'm so desperately needing are slowly declining. Because I'm unholy and defiant, smoking rollies of violence. I'm not going to church as much as I should because I'm lying-in sin. I try to pray and do good, but I always just end up lying to Him. I'm striving to repent but can't get the discipline or the strength. I keep breaking the commandments that Moses sent. The hardest one is adultery. I swear to God it's hard as an eggplant emoji to refrain when they approach me. How am I supposed to be when these sexy married women consult me? I'm tired of choking my chicken and I don't mean poultry. I dread the day their spouse sees my poetry and encroaches me. Maybe I should listen when my distant Christian counselor coaches me. But I felt like their marriages were invalid because of their religious preferences. So, I make duas to Allah as I'm caressing them and undressing them slowly. I love the Old Testaments but like King David I need concubines in my regimen and maybe a few good wives that I can love from behind in my regiment. You know I don't conform to most of these meagerly eastern standards. I love the love I get from these beautiful women but ye won't understand it.

I'm tired of my neighbor complaining to the landlord that he can't work, but he is collecting unemployment. How does that work, what a jerk. Maybe I just need someone to hug me, mentor me or coach me, but I keep giving them cold shrugs when they're trying to approach me. Even before this PLANdemic I distanced myself anti-socially. I wear shades in the day so hopefully, no one notices me. Because I'm hiding…. Personal questions have me 2nd guessing your intentions. I get too suspicious. So, I mostly reply by giving an awkward silence, mind your business. That spiritual awakening is helping me control my temperance, but please stay away from me, I'm emotionless and venomous.

My temperament keeps from seeming weak; it's hard to retreat from violence. Because we all know how that's going to go so, I try to be silent, but it seems like that's all they know and respect in my environment. You either check or get checked. I'm just sick and tired of this. Every day it never fails. It's another bill in the mail. I'm so overwhelmed. Oh no the devil won't prevail. I'm hopeless. Sometimes I wish I could just slit my own wrist, but the Holy Spirit won't let me, it always resisted it. Plus, my consciences thank God, he always stops it from being inflicted. I think about how my niece would have to grow up in Yonkers without my enriches.

But it does feel like it's just another big coincidence. That the bill collector's stalking every phone number that I get. This free WIFI keeps glitching. I can't even catch a flick on Netflix. My ex just flipped, trying to take everything back that she gave me but her herpes and syphilis. My next chick is too busy texting with her exes on a daily basis. It gets more hectic, she said she's pregnant with my baby. I'm about to go crazy!!! Allah, please save me. I'm about to flip! I'm hustling backwards, overspending all the cash that I get. I got one wrist in a handcuff and one foot in a casket. I'm just the shallowest fatherless old dirty bastard. My baby's mothers won't follow their visiting arrangements. If I don't buy them gifts, they'll make it strange to be around my kids. I'm too close to the edge. I'm trying to hold my pledge. I think I'd lose my mind if it wasn't attached to my head. Sometimes, I feel like I'm better off dead, underground six feet. Knowing that no one would utter a sound saying they'll miss me. The only time they call me is to get a ride or something from me, or when they need a favor otherwise, they'll quickly forget me. I'm tired of going to the gym or tucking my stomach in them pictures. I just wish I could be slimmer and eat what I want for dinner. I'm tired of being a loser. I hope I can be a winner. I'm tired of going to the casino just to get the free liquor. I know that the Tito's and this tequila is probably messing up my liver. But it makes me feel so good instead of those feelings that were bitter. I have so much resentment from my past relationships. I have no patience, waiting on vicious revenge karma to kick in. I'm paingry!!! Sometimes I wish that God could just end this quick. But then I see someone else in a worse predicament. That makes me grateful and thankful that I just pray. Hoping one day that all these feelings will just go away.

I'm paingry. Allah, please save me.

I'm paingry. Allah, please save me.

URGENT CARE DOESN'T CARE!!!

You ever wonder why the hospitals and urgent cares hire mostly foreigners to work in their private facilities? Why does the government give them grants that they wouldn't give to you or to me? Is it because it's cheaper to give them jobs so they wouldn't pay more money, to a citizen that worked hard in school for a PhD degree? Is it so they can train them with "obey or else" rules they're more likely to agree and adhere to, rather than get sent back to their home country prematurely in the next year or two? This is supposed to be urgent care!!! So why do I have to wait for 4 hours in this uncomfortable chair? Just for you to take my temperature and the other formalities to act like you care. But first the nurse must make sure my insurance works and is active and not impaired? Why does my insurance status matter the relief I get from my accident or the treatment I get when I come in here is the question I'm asking? But rather if I was richer or had better insurance my hospitality would be quicker, I learnt. I would even get seen first by the nurse because all they are concerned about is my money like a church. Why do I have to wait for my heart to burst and go berserk to get relief for you to really see that I'm hurt? Tell me please. Why do you take this as a game like I'm faking my pain in order to get narcotics? I could just go down the street and get it for cheap, I know they got it. You really need to stop it, all of us are not the same, so why do you treat me as if I'm toxic? Why do you use the word "narcotics" as if I'm a drug addict and I'm copping? I'm only coming here because it's like my only option. What does other people overdosing on street drugs have to do with this topic? What does that have to do with all this pain that I'm going through? Please try to explain to me I'm over here convulsing dude!!! Why would you prescribe medicines that I already have in my cabinet? That's backwards, why would I take ibuprofen for a broken bone and herniated disks is the question that I'm asking? I'm noticing you make me go through all the formalities just to call me back again for a follow up. That's just another check in the doctor's pockets for them to swallow up. Meanwhile my back is still in intensive pain, but now my blood pressure is rising because you're taking my life in vain. You should be more passionate. Butt, you act as if this doctor's visit is all about the digits than my pain. What is this that you're putting in my veins? I find it so hard to fathom that you're really happy that I came. It's like every time I come here the richer you get and the more that I'm going insane. It's more about my insurance and less about my cysts. I'm sick of it, this is inhumane and ridiculous. I can't even go to the hospital when I'm sick is sickening. These private hospitals and urgent cares are just a bunch of big businesses. Just a checkup to get them checks up and riches quick, and I'm sick of it!!

Merry Xxxmi$$

All I ever got for Christmas was dissed. No one care about me to even give me a gift. Luckily by God's grace I was gifted by Him. When they showed me their backs, He showed me His face and was always giving thanks. But meanwhile everybody was smiling, while I was mean, wilding, and childish. Acting out, broken, and hoping to get off my own island. Maybe it was because I couldn't let go of my foes and my woes. I was broke with no doe and still had the same clothes from a year ago. All my friends thought I was a weirdo. Because I was anti-social no matter where I go. I was so unapproachable I couldn't unclose my weary soul. No one cared, I know. I would've shown you my grief to open those wounds that you wanted to keep to yourself, because you can empathize and remember us guys that you could've helped with your wealth. But you chose to be greedy and not help the needy. You rather buy new clothes, coats, gifts, instead of feeding me. Not knowing what I was going through because you were too busy to see the omens or how I must've felt, you were too nonnegotiable. Yes, I was once hopeless though hoping that I could open a present, but instead I was treated like a peasant and repeatedly left stressing. Because every year it's been the same ole candy canes and gingerbreads and leftovers from the soulless dinners that they fed. But the rich got richer and didn't give to the poor, just got bigger on the Forbes, forgetting about the Lord. I often reminisce of being in that cold cell hoping I get a jingle bell and my name gets called for a single mail. Or at least a card but nahhhh!! It was the same ole Henny-less eggnogs, and generic gifts that I got to get but Alhamdulillaha. At the time it made no sense because my account had no cents, not even a penny in it. They were counting us all day but not putting us on the censuses. I couldn't even buy myself a gift. So, I had to sit and pray again for Jesus or Jehovah to come over and make their way in. They never came…. That was like praying for rain. So, you can miss me with this Christmas ish, every day is the same? To me this is just another holey day, a trick. For the pagans to get us to buy gifts, not a Holy day like my teachers depicted but just their laws of arithmetic. Jesus's birth can be celebrated every day when I pray. I hated when the system crossed me like a crucifix and sent me away. My holiday spirits were broken with juice and jinns and days filled with pains and bad memories of being dogged by them. You only make me think and relive it when you come around me being all jollying, I'm stressed. All I could think about is when my friends and family forgot about me again, I was oppressed. They left me in jail like I committed a homi or I raped a Dolly, pardon me, I'm sorry.... but I'm not sorry! Let me grieve. I'm trying to forget what the racist judicial system did to me because of my skin tint. All the holidays they $pent without me they forgot about me, having fun without me, left me to rot in pee. They didn't care so long as I wasn't there. At least I had my grandma, mom and sister that remembered me and cared. But I guess it was out of sight out of mind obviously. It's all good, I'm used to it, Thank God I had Coldca$h my PNC. Rico made sure I was paid in full on my commissary. Other than that, it wasn't merrily; those meals weren't heavenly. It wasn't fulfilling. It was the same old chicken and mash potatoes as I remembered partly. The cops used to lock us in just to have a Christmas party. I swear to God be, I was usually popped like a molly. But thanks to the great Allah he always got me. Inshallah I'll be greater later or hardly. But for now, I'll go crash into somebody's party and make a fool out of myself obnoxiously or probably end up drunk in a cell with a messed-up story to tell. Ignoring how I fell from the top and landing back in jail. Or committing a highway robbery dusted because my spirit is busted, like a sale. I know I'm just being a big contradiction, oh well!!!! At least I can judge myself. I know I'm probably going to hell, farewell. I didn't love myself. I got PTSD from being locked down so much, I felt so helplessly. I was emotionally stressed, overwhelmed plus I was mentally sick. So, let me be, so I can drown in my pool of piss and tears

. I'll be ok. I'll see you in the next new Jew year. But just mi$$ me with the Christmas ish. Especially since you have taken Christ out of it and it's all about a wish or gift. I don't got it to spend, my time is worth more than having it spent on buying a present. When it's supposed to be about God's presence. He presented Jesus for us to show us how to live. The time is of the essence. Please brethren, I'll let you celebrate peacefully but just don't tell me that it isn't fake like those trees that I hate to see. Let me be, I'm awake. Let me grieve and sip this honey Jack D Eggnog selfishly, like the grinch that stole my chick from me and left me helplessly. She also left me lonely, and the only thing that can soothe me is a Mariah Carey Christmas melody. But don't tell her please it may ruin my fantasy. I'm just an old dirty bastard that wants money handed to me. So, if you're not going to give it to me, then let me be. All I ever wanted for Christmas was to be with my family, but instead, all I got was stale food from a pantry. Bumps and bruises from macho men that weren't named Randy. Not even Elizabeth can understand me and my insanity candidly. The prison system mismanaged me. So, my bad if I wasn't good enough for you to gift me. Now I overstand the greed. So, mi$$ me with the Christmas ish please!!!

HOSPITALITY

I just got here!!! sir, why do I have to leave again? I'm supposed to get treated fairly regardless of the reason or my skin. I'm a United States citizen. But you're mistreating me like I'm an illegal immigrant or this is your tenement. Like I'm alien from Uranus, you're an anus, please show me some sentiment. Why can't you admit me at least, what's your name again? What's your benefit? Why are you acting like I'm a drug addict or a beastly man? I'm trying to refrain from static but the way you're treating me I can't. This makes me want to go crazy ham, dam! Is it because I'm just another brother with no insurance plan? Ma'am!!! Am I standing in France? If I am, pardon my French, bitch, but I am what I am. I know I may not be the best patient when I'm not at ease and I tend to get impatient but ma'am please!!! I need my pain to be relieved before you leave again like Shazam!!!

Why are you trying to inpatient me, in the can? I feel like shaqting a fool. But I know that's exactly what you want me exactly to do. Can you do something please? Don't you see that I'm hurting? This nonchalant treatment isn't appeasing, nor do I deserve this. By the way, I just observed with my own eyes that you served him. Is that on purpose? Does my skin color need a detergent? I can't wash out the color in your eyes in your higher learning. Is it because that I'm black, that I get treated like I'm an insurgent? You're violating my rights, no, I'm not high as these fee surges. I'm bursting, alright! I'm going to have to report this to OASIS, expeditiously as urgent, tonight! Why are you playing with my life, like it's worthle$$. Can I please speak to another nurse or a sergeant?

Why did you keep me in observation for four days? What are you observing anyway? Are you just waiting to see how my monetary option for your splurge is going to get you paid? Get out my way please. I need to speak to the doctor immediately. By the way, you're obligated by the state to treat me feasibly. Even as we speak, my injuries are starting to deplete me and make me weakly, can't you see! that I'm totally starting to fall asleep, sheesh!!! I'm aching and waiting just to be seen by another doctor or physician just to charge me weekly, please! Are you even listening to me? How much longer of this hypocrisy is going to take place Karen? Can I at least have my family come visit me so they can see my face before you put me into misery. I don't understand this, why are you so concerned about my insurance policy and how much money I make? You're going to get paid eventually anyway. How much more pain do I have to take, and why can't you do like you want me to do and wait. Wait, please! I can barely see, barely walk, and you're barely talking to me, why are you walking off? That morphine you gave me is starting to wear off. I'm peeved, the emotions on my sleeve I'm going to tear it off. You got my blood pressure rising, you can check my IV's but don't cut off my arteries like Verizon does to me. I keep losing my consciousness. I'm nodding in this condition critically, isn't it obvious that I need some type of special attention literally? I keep telling you my issues and the issue is that you're dissing me. Do you hear me? Are you even listening to me? I'm not trying to play the victim, but this is pitifully embarrassing and very vindictive. Why are you acting so malicious and offended? I'm not even being belligerent. You won't even feed me. You only merely gave me a turkey sandwich with no cheese. This is ridiculous. You're not even being conspicuous. When I asked for another one you called me greedy that's ungenerous miss.

Why did you lie on me? You said I was acting erratic and manically. When all I was trying to do was to get seen in a manner that I need. I'm starting to panic see. I don't like the way you're mishandling me, as if I'm panhandling in these streets. Where's your hospitality? I thought this was supposed to be an elite hospital. I say that candidly but you're not being sweet to me, miss answer me. You're trying to beat me like a vegetable, is it all about the capital like January 6? I bet if I was irrational or rich, I would've been checked in, if I had a check miss. I get the sense that you're a racist miss, why can't you speak to me? What are you documenting on your checklist secretly? Treat me equally please. My status shouldn't be a matter whether you're going to come correct miss, but why are you chauffeuring and shoving me to the next exit? You should treat everybody that comes in here with the same respect miss. I wish I never met

you, you're just a slave for a check. Why are the police checking my ID like I'm some sort of murder suspect?
 I'll bet you every penny, that's because of the color of my flesh. But I can't help the melanin skin that I'm in, but that doesn't make me a felon miss. What type of sewer you fell in? Don't they see that I'm here in distress and not under arrest? Don't they see me hooked up to this IV or the EKGs on my chest? This systematic racism is unpatriotic circumcision at its best. Why are they more concerned with checking my jail records and testing to see if I was drinking? I wasn't even driving, nevertheless being reckless. Why are they asking me all these inappropriate invasive questions? What are they thinking? Trying to get me to testify on him to make a confession? While I'm lying on my hospital deathbed dying. I don't know how I'm holding my composure and being compliant. You want to discharge me because I look like I'm violent? Is this all because I am black with blues and violet? or is it that I have no health insurance or that I'm not a prestigious client that you won't help me to your best capacity stop being defiant. If I wasn't depleted, I would've torn this hospital into pieces, but I chose to retreat and keep my peace, so please be decent. But although I'm going to put my words onto a thesis I rather go against the urge to go berserk and turn this visit into feces. This hospital is so inhospitable, disrespectful, and very indecent. I want to go crazy, and have you call the whole police precinct and wild out like Larry Davis, just to let them know that I mean it and I ain't playing. Why are you giving me the business like I was mean and inconvenient? I could get shot up or locked up for a century of weekends. So, I'm going to just turn my cheek like Jesus did, unwillingly and impetuously. Like a priest I prayed trying to refrain from them taking my freedom. While they preyed on my fees and visas I laid weakened. I knew God would make a way he always

answers when I seek him. I'm just an image that made it through them fogs up in Beacon.
 When I was hidden in the mountains up in Schitt's creek then. So, I knew I could count on him again. I always beseech him. He's so dependently splendid I was supposed to meet death then. I was pronounced dead according to them but instead I'm alive and still breathing. Thank God that I somehow managed to survive death row like Dr. Dre with my heart beating. With minimal brain damage Alhamdulillah.

mayday mayday. I didn't panic because I knew I would see better days. Jibril is real, he escorted me back when I was trapped in that car crash. My chances to live were slim. I could've died in that shady aftermath, but God had a plan and somehow, I managed to survive that jam. So now I'm going to eat humble pie right out of his hand. That's why I didn't go insane in this hospital because I can! But I'm going to be good and put my pride to the side and be a man. Thank God, He never aborted me like y'all doing to me ma'am.

 Thanks to the members from YFD and ambulance for giving me another chance. Giving me the Heimlich and fighting to save my life. I will always pay homage to them because they saved me twice. My back was sprained and impaired backed against that chair, the car flipped in the air on the Sprain I was gasping for air… Then I woke up to doctors and nurses trying to get me to sign these dotted lines in cursive. So, I can fill up their pockets and purses. I started spazzing out because that got me so nervous. I was so obnoxious and cursing that I had to get carried out like a knot was in my cervix, but I do not have a cervix. I was probably a hot mess and a nerve wreck, and the nurses probably really didn't deserve it. But I was kind of delirious. I'm sorry if I took it

seriously and blurted. I had just previously literally by inches just missed my turn of death
. All I can remember is the tremors and them jerking my neck. Like sign this paper. I was half dead and all they were worrying about was me signing a check!!!!

I was like no way, you wouldn't treat me like this if I was beige. They had me enraged. They gave me a Haldol shot and locked me up in a cage like a Rott. They even called the cops to try to make them give me a false charge of trespassing. But when I started recording their actions, they all started adjusting their badges. Then they had me kicked off the property, without treating me properly. I thought this was a hospital!!! Where is the hospitality??? Then they gave me some generic discharge papers with instructions to take some ibuprofen and Robitussin. For three spinal herniated disks, a dislocated shoulder, and a major concussion? Do they think that I'm super hueman or something? or that I was going to just sit back and relax and not say nothing? If it wasn't for my family coming to visit me and making complaints. I would've just been a John Doe eventually or probably arraigned in the clink.

ME AND MY CANE

When I met you, I admit my first thought was I didn't need this stick. Then I slipped… lost my strength then had to put my pride to the side and walk like a crip. I never felt that way in my life, it didn't take long until I made you like my thot or my wife. In those dark gloomy nights, you were my light. You really gave me stability and tranquility. You gave me hope in my new plight. You were my crutch in the clutch that helped me up those flights of stairs. You were right there. It was clear we had a mad tight affair. Which was weird, but during those days you were my fourth leg. You held me stable like a table. You gave me courage and the will. You were ready when I wasn't abled. Steel, for me you stood still.

For real you were always there like bills from my cable, I really wasn't capable. At first, I was so shy I didn't know why or what to make of you, I was unstable. I was worried about being labeled disabled. But you were my cane. The one who never let me down the drain when I was drowning in disdain. You always stayed around, never clowned me or left me in vain. You walked with me through the snow and even helped me in the rain. Even though those who was close to me forgotten my name. You never left me or let me rot in this pain. I must admit you gave me strength when I wanted to die, and when I cried like a snitch. You loved me however in any weather, whether I was broken or rich. You helped me build up to get fully emotionally equipped. When the time is right, and my mind is right. I'm going to do something nice. You helped me find life and never crossed me like they did Christ.

Just me and my cane me and my cane.
Just me and my cane.
Just me and my cane me and my cane
Just me and my cane.

When I had no doe or no goals you wouldn't let me go, even though I was slow you held me down like ten toes you would never fold. oh no you'll never do that. A real friend is all I ever wanted but I never ever had. If truth be told you helped me diddy bop, made me stronger.

Helped me stash my trees from the city cops when they were on us. You warned me with your GPS. You made sure you never seen me stressed. You held me down when my knees needed a rest, especially in those long lines in that CVS. You helped me receive them checks. When I was lonely you kept me company, even when I had no food or money or when I was rude and ugly. But you'd never judged me. You knew that I was in pain, you were my cane-panion, who kept it true and trusted in me. Even when they busted me, you never folded or told. You kept me standing tall through it all I never shuffled my feet on them roads.

Just me and my cane me and my cane
Just me and my cane.
Just me and my cane me and my cane
Just me and my cane.

Even though I wasn't a typical cripple, you didn't get all incidental when my knees used to pop like a pimple. You rocked with me to the beat like an instrumental. You supported me, never aborted me like all of them bimbos. Even though I limped slow, you consorted with me until the end bro. Although, they said my chances to walk was in limbo and thrown out the window you didn't go. Even when I was losing, you always wanted me to win
though. You're always gonna be remembered by me.

You defended me from my enemies and even them many attempt botched robberies. It even gotten me out of poverty. When I couldn't walk or talk properly, you helped me retain my first property. You probably got me wealthy, because you were the only one who ever felt me. That could understand my plans when no one else wanted to be bothered by me or help me. When I had no helping hands you knelt with me. Prayed to Allah with me. You made salaats with me. You were more than an object to me, My BFF obviously. I could always lean on thee, you never switched up on me or lied to me. Whether I was in the penitentiary or a free man like Morgan, you wouldn't let them put me in a morgue. You overstand my ideology. I knew that eventually I could count on you, and you would ride for me. When I was all alone in my misery, you'd never look at me pitifully. I knew if it came down to it you would die for me, literally.

Just me and my cane, me and my can
Just me and my cane.
Just me and my cane, me and my cane
Just me and my cane.

SORRY, I'M NOT SORRY

No more lies, no more cries. No longer do their treachery and envy hide in disguise. I can see clearly now through the bullspit with my 3rd eye. The wool is no longer pulled over my eyes. I'm awake and alive, but why do you look so surprised when I realized the real from the lies? Yet, you still connive and conceal all your crimes. You've been taking advantage of my kindness. You thought it was a weakness. Now I can understand it. I must've been blinded by love to perceive it. Now my eye lids can see clearly, 2020 vision repaired me. You were so used to me being intoxicated and impaired incoherently to not see my Holy deity. See rarely did I ever fall victim. I must've been drugging and slipping. I knew it was only a matter of time before I would bounce back into rhythm. I will now make better decisions. You used to rely on what I would say and twist it. just like this racist system. You will also know your real friends when you have no cents, because most of them will turn their back on you when things get intense. I remember them hills in Schuylkill, where 75% of the gents would squeal. I kept it real behind that fence, even though events of my appeals were nil. I didn't know what exactly, but I knew Allah had a plan for me. I was made in his image but didn't quite understand his Deen. But I knew snitching wasn't an alternative. Even though I was wrongly convicted I still never burnt a bridge. I just knew I had to make stronger decisions. Allah Akbar, God is great no matter which I may say. He knows my intentions are affirmative in my ways. One day we can be here and the next day we could vanish. That's why I pray every day and hope God can understand it. I'm not perfect but I worship and came to learn quick. That without him, my life was unmanaged, frantic, and deterrent. So sorry I'm not sorry, I give Allah all the glory. He has the most importance to me. He's not finished with my story....

P.C.P

Please stop controlling me.
Can't you see that you're really taking hold of me.
Possibly I can't stop on my own. I need help.

Please leave me alone and go bother somebody else.
Can't you see all the pain that I have felt.
Putting poison in my body refraining from proper health.

Please leave me be because my mind is in a chronic unsynchronized malady.
Can't you see the ruin in totality? My mind has embraced enough fatalities.
Principalities undermine my punitive decisions and childish mentalities.

Passing thoughts, like my memory I'm lost in this makeshift.
Captured in a complacent matrix of fakeness.
Partaking myself in Ill-advised situations.

Prisons filled with prisms of invisible women.
C-o's screaming get in.... my cell again.
Phones with jail tones of over-estrogenic men, I failed again.

Probably ain't going to make it because I'm out here insane and running naked, I need a mentor.
Cold like December but tomorrow I won't remember.
Putting myself in positions to be sitting in that House in Virginia, with the church mouses yelling timber!

Peacefully I'm not, but I want to put my mind at ease so lose the excuses bruh.
Can't you see!!! I have limited control over you and lucid Lucifer?
Powerless over the decision that I choose to use. I'm used up.

Pathetic
Cruel
Prosthetic

Pools of waterless deserts.
Cactuses
Pricking my soul, promising things I'll never deserve.

Poetry is like the sweetest hazardous
Cravings of an addict... maybe I'm attracted.
Phosphorite acids leaking through my fabrics.

Probably messed up
Chances that I could not see.
Professing my confessions unclearly.

Peter said that I'm great and that I'm chosen.
Can't you see the third eye that you are closing.
Priorities in my life you are withholding.

Paralyzed by those potent mint leaves I was smoking.
Convulsions from seizures how can I be a leader if I'm dozing.
Paramedics repeatedly reprieving me from overdosing.

Powerful.
Controlling.
Persuasive.

Powerless
Contagious
Problematic

Please
Call
Police

Pancreas
Constricted
Paternally

SAMHSA's National Helpline – 1-800-662-HELP (4357)
SAMHSA's National Helpline is a free, confidential, 24/7, 365-day-a-year treatment referral and information service (in English and Spanish) for individuals and families facing mental and/or substance use disorders.

HUNGER PAINS

I'm sick and tired of dieting and living like a bulimic. I just want to eat what I want when I want to eat it. My stomach is hungry right now and I just want to feed it. I don't care about what you think about me when I'm feasting. I want some smothered lamb chops with macaroni with three different cheeses. I need some turkey bacon in my collard greens and a sweet kiwi iced tea mix. I want some layered meaty lasagna with garlic bread that's very buttery without having to count the calories on a treat that makes me smack my teeth, I'm hungry! Those carrot sticks and rice cakes don't really satisfy my appetite or my greed. I just want some Chinese chicken wings with shrimp fried rice, please. Not just a half a bite I want to bust it all down, I'm tired of living my life unpleased

I got the munchies now. I want a large apple pie with ice cream on top, Moose tracks to be exact. Then I'll probably get the itis after my arthritis kicks in. Then I'll take a nap. There's nothing quicker than Snicker with a Pepsi for a snack I can't avoid. Chocolate-covered almonds bring me joy. Chips Ahoy bring the noise. Even though I'm 2 scoops of fruit loops from diabetes I want to eat what I want. I want to eat something sweet with a Venti Caramel Macchiato with two extra pumps.

I want to wake 'n' bake to some strawberry banana vanilla pancakes with a big cheesy omelet with savory sausages from down south that my favorite auntie makes. I just want to eat without these skinny jeans showing what I got in my pockets, nothing!!!

I want to fit in this slim shirt without worrying about if I sneeze, I'm going to pop a button. Sometimes, I just want to be free, gloat and eat like a glutton. I'm so sick and tired of putting my stomach on punishment. I'm tired of spending countless and profitless hours at the gym for nothing. To come back home exhausted to put a TV dinner in the microwave oven. I just want German chocolate cake without having to take a pill that's not in my budget or having to feel like Dr. Phil's watching me tucking in my belly button.

I'm tired of trying to impress the same people that oppress me. No longer do I care about them thinking less of me. I was feeling much better being chubby, eating right out the pot. I rather you hate me for who I am instead of loving me for who I am not. I'm happy at the buffets, eating all I want for brunch on Sundays. I can't wait to be an official Ihopper or eat a triple whopper on a Monday. I just want to have fun and run away, because I'm tired of eating like a vegan. I want some lobster tails with shrimps and pumpkin pie, gleaming with pecans.

I don't care how you look at me, my edible fudge brownies make me content. Those warm Cinnabon's with a cold glass of almond milk are legit. I love them crispy creme pastries. They make me the opposite of hangry. I know my waist trainer's going to shame me. Butt I want a snack box from KFC and maybe some Popeyes with sweet potato pie or a 3piece from Kennedy's. That will make me happy and upbeat. I'm tired of eating all these salads that's healthy. Tofu and Quinoa are boring. I can't keep up with six meals. I'm tired of eating those small portions. All that does is make me raid the fridge with the munchies at four in the morning. Trust me, I be going all in. The food is calling. I'm trying to change my number and stick to exercises and a strict diet to help tame my hunger. I gave up every time I tried it, but I got to change my habits. Now I eat to live and don't live to eat, but sometimes I do miss eating like a savage.

CHAPTER 4

Motivation 4
The nation

PRICELE$$

The greatest gifts you can ever give.
Is love
Life and good advice.
The most valuable things
You can't buy
They don't come with a price.

C.O.P.

Clean-up Our Place.
We both have seen enough hate
We know it's only a job you enrolled to take
But it's a choice that you chose to make
How can you win trust from US at this rate
When your charges are trumped up or fake
Pun intended...
So please can y'all deal with some equality
When you on the chase or when you follow me
Can you have moral and integrity principalities
In placed and not judge US by our race, honestly
Can you have a fair judgment and adjust your hate
do not Judge US, when you show up to our place
do not condemn and have a grudge on your face
Just looking to bust us to bust up our day

C our pain
Can you not look at US, as we are indifferent
than your own children have some feelings
Use love over hate, consider us as your siblings
We all make mistakes, but we're not all villains
Please make that small sacrifice I love my life
Give US justice and not just the ice
Don't take the only husband from my wife
My kids need me they might get lonely at night

Civilization Over prosperity.
I know it's hard coming in unknown territories
and communities where crime is terribly gory
Where it is high in violence and fatalities
But please, can we stop these police brutalities
Cease the immunities and the notorieties
That you only give to other higher societies
Let every overseer officer respond with the ability
and the tranquility to accept their responsibilities
and to account for his or her own actions
when they shoot and kill an unarmed Blackman
suspected of a crime that never happened
Stop using our bodies as target practices

Clear Ones Principalities.
Please think about the trauma of all our families
before your fingers squeeze those triggers
Please consider that we're not all fiends and niggers
Please follow all the protocols and the policies
before you go pick up that gun, pop and squeeze
the life out our lungs, stop and breathe
think before you act or you have the need
to make another Blackman not see his seeds
Have them growing up with no pops or deeds

Communication Over Pulling guns.
We are not your enemies, even though some of US is bugged
Think before you aim and want to bang your gun
gavel like a judge, death travel with them slugs
Some of US is just trying to eat or get some funds
because we live in intensive poverty-stricken slums
We are just trying to make some money to feed our families
so, they can sleep in peace, understand me please!!!
Before you RIP me, my hands is in the air
Get the hate out your eyes to see me, play fair
before you execute me I'll rather take a chair
don't shoot me and leave my fate in despair
so my family don't grieve, or see me on TV aired
on the news shot dead in the Square, lead in my hair
Please, my knees are on the pews, act like I was you… here!
Have a different view before your bullets spew without a care

Create Objective Protection.
Here take my keys, my cars, and my money I get it
Just don't take my life I don't have a weapon
Our issues will never get right with this aggression
My nephew and niece need me for their lessons
to teach and lead them, this is just your profession
You're supposed to protect my freedom, not neglect it
Don't shoot!!!
all I have on is this hoodie and sweats, I'm sweating!
That's not a gun it's only a woody, an erection
I hope you're not stressed or vexed at my complexion
Don't shoot!!!
that is just a cross on my necklace
It represents a reminder for Gods Ordinary Directions.
Don't shoot!!!
and make my mom stress again,
because I'm not only her son I'm also her best friend

Cooperation Over Persecutions.
Stop taking your job personal with oppression
Please don't shoot I wasn't driving reckless
That smell is coming from my prescribed medicines
It's not a cause for you to probably arrest me again
You can't check my vehicle here's my registration
Don't violate my 4th amendment so brazen
It's not probable that I'm committing a crime
because of the scent that you smell, I'm fine!
That's just an excuse to be a nuisance and intrusive
Please don't shoot, no I didn't do it… don't do it!

Care Overall Programs
That's not a gun, weapon, or dope in my hand you, see?
It's just another mistaken misperception of identity
Not all of us are a danger to and/or a menace to society
We are not all criminals with subliminal criminality
I'm holding up both hands as high as they can be.
So please use your intelligence and not negligence
and abide by some kind of piety that you represent
Is that a badge of honor or a license to kill me?
Do you have any type of empathy or dignity?
Do you ever feel guilty? Where is your integrity?
Arresting me for a quota, your hands are filthy, verily
So before you bury me in these streets, unfairly
Let's see if we can achieve some peace, spare me
I understand that you have a mission and a job to do
You're a cop
I'm an alleged criminal, but I have no problem with you
All that I'm asking you for is peace and mutual respect
and for you to please! Take your foot off our necks!!!

OPERATION LOCKDOWN

All I see is thieves misleading the blind and our country's crime being inclined. If it wasn't for the police, I would've achieved in my prime. They kept stealing my shine, putting my time in recline. I could've been in the NFL or the NBA plenty of minds, but my dreams and hopes hoaxed that mission of mine. It all went up in smoke by that prison time they gave me. I was just a baby. Young, reckless, and crazy so it didn't faze me. My future was thrown away because of one dumb decision that I chose to make on a bad day which froze my fate. I graduated from high school high on Friday just to get locked up Saturday. Every day felt like a Sunday there isn't no holy days or holidays in their tiers as the pagans portrayed. My hopes and fears were drowned in my tears as things became drear, I was afraid. They made it clear that I was going to be down for some years. My people left me without a chair, so I had to stand up. They counted me out. life isn't fair; I had to man up. I was thinking how God can just leave me there with my peers, this is weird. We all were in there, teenagers with criminal careers. Yeah, most of us were the same color with different complexions. But I didn't see any of us there with charges of mass destruction weapons, just selling drugs as a profession. But maybe our penises were the real guns they were trying to silence. They are non-tolerant of Indigenous ingenuous geniuses. Let me be quiet. Six out of ten alleged crimes that were committed were domestic or nonviolent but in the system you're guilty until proven innocent unless you had a check or a bond bailsman. Otherwise, you were arrested then committed to an asylum. They are taking US kids from our cribs then putting us in crazy predicaments. It is what it is where I live. Nasty Nas and Nostradamus predicted this. What about adolescents. How are they going to live through this without the lessons we should have given to them? How are they going to understand in this wretched uncivilized nation of mayhem? In which, their HIStory is tainted. How are they going to make it without going through Allah's college of greatness. Slavery isn't abolished, it's just polished by fake scholars and racists. Peace to the Polish, Patriots and Asians but how are our sister's going to raise a

Blackman in this nation? They tried to F-bomb Farrakhan like they did Saddam in his own land. The nation of Islam is lam, they put the iron cuffs on their onyx hands. They put bullets in their brains and not just hollow tips but those God damned K2 spliffs and wet dust blunts, take a whiff. They got them poisonous potions and liquors they were swallowing. How can we all be law Biden or trust a Trump in this Parliament? When they're racked up and backed up by the same Amerikkkan racists. They don't want us to make it, apparently it is hatred. It's messed up Dan, but they'll rather leave US naked in this cold world, burnt up. The KKK is still burning up black churches trying to hurt us. The big willies still lynching our children and buying up all of them buildings. Gentrificating our generation but we're still not learning or willing. To them crackers your million slave master dollars is worthless. They're turning the projects into condos for foreign Europeans to purchase. Why are these blatant racists emerging? Out of nowhere they just appeared determined with a purpose. Why is the cost of living so high as the calories from Mickey D's? I'm just being earnest and honest when I speak but you steel won't listen to me. Are we still going to eat our fast-food fast and not save our currencies nor return or buy black as we are doing currently? It's not funny but they're laughing at US, we're still buying overpriced fashion. While they're sitting back cashing in not caring about the markets crashing in. While we're helping them invest in their seeds from our indefinitely shopping sprees, we're stressed, depressed, and smoking cancerous cigarettes monotonously. R.I.P. to Malcom X we must have forgotten his speech. How can I watch the TV that's watching me? Obviously, Moses had to part the sea to get away from the Pharisees. Which is symbolic to what we must do in Amerikkka for US to be financially free. Moses also gave the commandments that he was handed, but most of us are too fly or high to understand it. Probably because it's not like the same languages on the radio the stations are playing. Those chants of emotionalized ill-advised statement sayings. Telling US, to kill kill kill. Prostitute your souls to pay them bills bills bills. They want US to be nil and pop them pills pills pills, so we can be dumb and numbed and not see them are coming for real real real. There are too many ills ills eels in the ocean making it harder to focus. Just by giving them notice that we are the chosen is making them go bogus. That should be the notion for us to believe and achieve, but first we must be free physically and mentally for US to succeed.

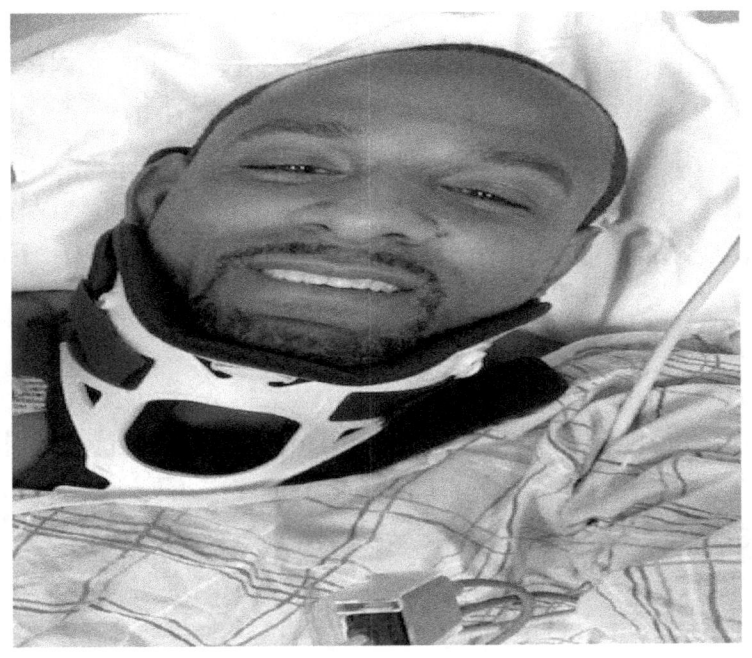

MIRACLE WHIP

I could have been a paraplegic if I didn't believe in Allah. I'm glad I conceded as you can see from the incident in that car. I was conceited, my mistakes I couldn't see them. I was blinded by a mischievous fate and my mental state was devious. It took eight brave men to save him out of that deep ditch but I'm okay, Amen. You can say that again. All praises to Him. I'm not trying to get spiritual, but it was a miracle how that whip after 3 flips, a spin or two was an experience that was livable. I was able to come out of that accident and be lyrical.

It's God's grace that I'm living through. It's vivid proof that you see me here with you and not in a funeral. He saved me for a reason that's a clear view. I glorify his name even through the hunger and the pains. I came from the same grain as you. I'm just glad to be breathing. I'm just a messenger in his image or rather a genius but my path was ingenious. So put down those weapons unless you're fighting for something with meaning. Like your rights, insights and under achievements. Our brothers and sisters really need it. Your help is needed for them to succeed in the land of the demons. Please have a good evening and enjoy your weekend. I'll see you soon Inshallah if He deems it. I thank God for giving you the ability to even read this.

NO RETREAT OR SURRENDER TO HIS HORRIBLE AGENDAS

Forget the haters and the naysayers. Inshallah I'm going to wake up every day and strive to be draped up in gold like them Lakers. I guess I'm the one chosen to display what I have to say in words in a Kingish way like the all-time Gr8 with a Nip of hustle flavor but never forgetting to praise my savior. Every day, like Ramadan I fast and Jihad on my past behaviors. My bad, I'm only a hueman that isn't perfect, but I do worship everyday sun. So, I could never be frozen like an icicle because I'm official like a referee's whistle. That's a fact my nizzo. I never gave up on me, not even a little. I made it reign from a drizzle. I can't quit. But as I sit, I just laugh back hah, because they want me to sell crack crack. So, I can go back back. But I will never be in that same trap trap. In fact, I'm a King's king that don't crack crack. I'm black, black, that's a fast Mack fact. Never again will I ever fall for that crap jack. Devil step back back! They're trying to buy up all our habitat, to clean up where they placed all the ones with bad habits at. I'm striving to not let them crackers do that that while surviving in the maddest environment.

Where they are trying to zap our retirements zap zap to be honest your honor that was my last batch. I tried to quit before my prime hit but got popped in the process, tap tap. Knock, knock on wood, this time I will sure do good and get past the past. I want to provide a way for the kids to not have to go back through them crack traps. So, they can maintain in their brains that they're so much smarter than that and can go harder. If they can just adjust their partners that don't want them to fly above the gardens. Pardon me, as I stand in my square with a square in the corner of Madison with no squadron. Doing what God wants me to do because he's awesome and his plans for me, I'm part of. I know the devil doesn't play fair and wants to send me back to jail so I can stay there. He wants me to go postal, no mail because he really doesn't care I could tell. He just wants to use me, abuse me, and confuse me. Then like usually he'll disappear. But I will never retreat or surrender to his horrible agenda. God made me a winner and an honorable contender

Gr8

Gr8ness...2 4's equals 8. He built with positivity and destroyed negativity stay awake. Reading is fundamental when you're expanding knowledge. It's like adding funds to your mental. The black mamba snaked his way to greatness overcoming hood rituals. He had a unique great mind state. He was a different breed from the gate. From Philly, home of the cheesesteaks, and Jellybean's estate. He chose to rose above the bitter streets and be great like you and me could be if you could relate and end the hate immediately.

Gr8ness... He started on a bench and became a goat. He played his role and drove to achieve more than those bricks that paved those roads. He picked and rolled with Shaq and dunked on the haters who tried to block him. Bolo'd Mutombo's he never feared his competition that tried knocking him. He never pretended to be any other than the representation of his trophies and plaques. Winning was his only option in fact he did just that.

Gr8ness...They didn't want him to succeed but he fought every day to not let that be. Figuratively and statistically, he was literally beyond being an NBA MVP. Black Mamba on them bombaclattas that envied he. He never switched up on his teams, just bombed 3's like TNT.

Gr8ness...He was always striving. 2-4 was a wise man that used his knowledge and ambition. He was driven to shoot his way out of the streets with his talents that God has given to him from within. He practiced every day and believed in his culture. He rose above the vultures like an Eagle from Philly. He crossed over from those streets to Italy to play ball because jellybean knew how cold and jelly the streets can be.

Gr8ness...He chose to change his strange ways and became a gr8 contender. He made a mistake in Denver but didn't let that be his fatal destiny for one cold night in December. There are always two sides to a token. He made a way for his family, decided, and chose them. He was humbled he let his game do the talking which was outspoken. A laker that was golden one of the 75 greatest ever chosen. He always kept a smile, but his game was not joking. He was never known not to shoot his shot if he was open. R.I.P. to Gigi. She was destined to be as great as he. Persistently he worked hard to put in twenty years being great consistently. That's two decades of sportsmanship and positive quotes. He paved his path and will live past 2020, he will forever be the goat.

Gr8ness...He didn't want to be like Mike; he wanted to create his own hype. RIP King Shinobi a trophy should be honored in his name tonight. He was the ultimate prototype. He will forever be illuminated, an omen in the sky. He didn't fold or cry when it got rough, he chose to ride. He brung gr8ness to the game. First time on the ballot in the hall of fame the Gr8 Kobe Bryant remember his name.

REVOLT OR VOTE

We can't breathe, please take your knees off our necks, show us some respect or you know what's coming next. There's too much chatting, that is only taking us backwards. They heard our voices already, now we need to start projecting some actions. As a matter of fact, we need to stop relaxing and be more proactive in our approach to injustices tactics. I'm tired of asking for budgets and equality. For what we can clearly see they're not budging when it comes to our dearly needs. Unless it's for their benefits, we must put an end to this and force them to reap the repercussions from their racial injustice implements. The republicans and democrats are puppets of the government. Then when they get into the office they just hush and button their lips. We must make our votes count before they miscount the votes. Then we'll be stuck in it, for another four years in a conjunctivitis corruption. Blinded by the light, right in front of your faces can't see what's inside the chalice. Whatever way you have it, the challenge is to pick the lesser poison in the ballots. That is in conjunction with demanding results and their production. The red or blue pill consumption is still hard to stomach. We have to make them do something. Make sure you do the math and don't go by confused assumptions. They'll always conceal their intentions when they're on your television pulpitting for a position in any political junction. It won't be that obvious. The only way to stop their dumbness and dominance and for our issues to be prominent is to cause an abruption. Choosing a side with lesser corruption to open the doors that are compressed by eruption. Pick your poison, but make sure that your decision is picked with precision. So that your votes count when they count the votes whichever state you live in. Just don't stand there and do nothing, show your position before our power diminishes. Knowledge is infinite.

RED WHITE AND THE BLUES

There's a cold war going on outside that no black man is safe from, they say our chances of dying is 48 to 1. They are lying, falsifying, and trying to control the population by black men dying. Meanwhile they are having babies crazy multiplying. They're mistreating US bad, especially when we get to them hospitals where them doctors are full of bull spit, signing every death certificate with covid even if they weren't sick. This is all part of the script that comes with spiritual and nuclear warfare. They're killing blacks swiftly by any means all year, be aware. They have 5G towers planted everywhere and when we protest it, they're sending troops that's itching to shoot with heavy gear. Take note of this. Meanwhile we're in this PLANdemic they're using fear, and the government is highly prepared. At night I used to hear helicopters chopping dropping something in the air, it's getting weird. Their mission is to divide and conquer US to despair. Be aware. They're trying to control our population until we all just disappear. In this real-life low-key genocide so many black men have died, while the oppressors multiplied multiple times am I lying??? We lost Hank Aaron, Black Mamba, Black Panther, then Biz took his last breath, as well as Black Rob and DMX. So, when I wake up, I'm stressed to turn on the bad news to see who's next. Not that I forgot to mention all our black queens and kings that have passed from covid or the vaccines or the mental health collapse or the tax liens, for all those who couldn't afford to pay their mortgages now they got to put their stuff in storages it's not good in the hood, it's horrific. All I want to know is "what's going on?" Marvin's been gone and it's still a prevalent relevant song.

They tried to blind US and mislead US in the news to keep US confused, and off balanced, clueless, and subdued they know what to do. Lying to the public, having our so-called celebrities endorse it for an endorsement using them as puppets. Then they got rid of trump/pence when the whistle blowers blew in them trumpets, but now it's back to the dumbness we can't win for losing in this corruption. If black lives matter. Then let's move in a way that matters and do what we must do to get out of this disaster, because marching isn't changing their habits. Peaceful protesting isn't stopping the cops Glocks from blatting and shattering families causing instant insanity in captions. We can't do no good is what it seems, to the cops that show up at the scene like Freddy Kruger with the Ruger to kill your dreams. Now they're shooting children and women too. To them we're all just black strangers. We look the same with big targets on our backs. They're shooting their shots like vodka with no chaser, all you hear is pop!!! They make sure nothing is left in the chamber, like an injustice judge then it's US against US. If Miss Liberty is blindfolded, then how can we trust in her?

It's going to take more rioting and looting to stop the shootings. They're polluting our hood. They know exactly what they're doing and how to do it. They use divide and conquer clauses and the laws of Sun Tzu, the Art of War. Well, I reside in Yonkers, and I got a gun too and I am not scared to draw like Davinci better them than me. They're not going to make me a memory like they did to Kennedy. I'm blazing back, rather than to be in my drawers on the floor and them playing taser tag. Aiming at my penis, so I can't be made a dad. I'm not a genus but I do know when you go, there's no making it back. Besides God's not ready to have me lay in the back of that Cadillac or Chevy, that's a fact. So, I go hard and heavy. I'll rather renegade for my peoples that they're shooting. They're subduing and arresting US. Miseducating, fastfooding, and polluting the rest of US. Unless we step it up and change, aint nothing going to come. I vividly remember Sam Cook singing this when I was young. Then I turn on the TV just to see a cop stop breath from pumping into his lungs, just don't stand there do something hun.

My intellectual guessing is the oppressing will never stop until they take the aggression away from the racist cops. Then they must change the systematic racism in the courthouse and the disparity in the sentences that's being brought out. They have our men and women in vicious prison cycles. Imagine bidding, living, and visiting those who look just like you. All overseen by people that don't like you but would try to lie to you or try to buy you with tax credits and stimuluses while they're trying to evaporate the indigent. They're also trying to emasculate the citizens that's why we got to get it in; them votes and pick the lesser poison even though this is all just a hoax. I say we have to revolt and overthrow this whole racist system, and I propose that we need to give the Supreme Court's term an ending. Because we're not winning once the case goes to them, we're 89% defenseless, so it's senseless to keep giving in to them. We're in a war that we are never going to win unless we do something different, mentally load the clips, which is symbolic to being holistic.

  We must make them change the racist system by getting their positions, its US against them doesn't trust the government. They see it the same way but in a capitalistic view. To be aware is to be alive, don't wait until it happens to you.

CHAPTER 5 BROTHER LOVE

Love ♥

Peace ☮

And

Happiness

HEY BLACKMAN

Hey Blackman.... Let me help you get up out of that quicksand. Its ok I overstand, here grip my hand. We're in the midst of the wretched plans from the Willie lynchings, the Jim Crow laws and the Ku Klux Klan. They want us in prison. They want us to be away from our beautiful women. They want to keep our minds imprisoned, blindfolded, and not listening to the visions of what Martin Luther King Jr, Malcolm X and Huey P was mentioning. They want us to keep watching Hella vision, to compel our vision and watch us back through the same television. That tv is smarter than what you're thinking!!! Watching and clocking you, can't

you see it blinking? They want us popping Clozapine's, Xanax's, and Perc's,
 depending on big Pharma and Aunt Jemima so we could vanish our worth. They want us to instill drugs in our babies at birth, so they can be sentenced and addicted to the devilish curse.

Hey Blackman.... They want US to export and exploit our women, have them bust it open for a slave master emblem. They want US to have our sisters stripping to our music along with their prides in every way I ain't lying like Lucious. They don't want us to have an empire, which is ludicrous in my eyelids. There's a liquor store on every corner where I live.

Hey Blackman.... They're trying to buy up all the land and the properties here. They want us all on welfare so we can't do well here but who the hell cares. They'll sell your social security number for 12 shares. While we're too busy trying to be jazzy their filling up their banks and living in Bellaire.

Hey Blackman.... It's time to put down that Belvedere it's a different world out here. Those drugs got you bugged and living without a fear. Jasmin trying to be a guy and Kadeem trying so hard not to have too much pride that he keeps all her cries inside. They even got black magic spells on Aphrodite, and for forty dollars you can more than likely get laid tonight if you ask her right. Hennessy is the aphrodisiac cognac, and we all have an appetite for destruction. They're breaking us fast with no repercussions, we're plummeting. John is tricking our sisters with Uncle Sam being their pimps. They want US to sell our queens cookies trying to make them famous like Amos selling their anus in the dark internet back pages where only her fans are cool with it, because it pays the rent. As well as their soul just to go bankrupt in their accountability but you ain't really feeling me you rather shush me by killing me.

Hey Blackman.... They want US to feed our seeds fast food, then wonder why they have bad moods and attitudes at their schools. That's preparing them to be a better fool on a pedestal learning tools to a trade that they'll never do. They're subconsciously training you to second you and overvalue that cash that's in your hand to come first and you 2nd to you. The moment you quit is the second you lose. Just guess what their most effective weapon is?... it's you

Hey Blackman.... Together we stand divided and we fall. Hey Blackman.... I'm talking to y'all

Veteran's Day

Peace, to all the veterans you're a better man than me I appreciate you fighting for our country, you never ran from defeat. You deserve all the glory like Denzel, if it wasn't for you, I wouldn't have been able to excel. I respect and honor you, for going to war for me your service made me a free man like Morgan, true story. I'm glad we could lean on you. Your sacrifice was important to me. I hope the sun gleams on you and your light forces fortunes on me. It takes guts and heart to depart overseas. You made it possible for US to be able to overachieve. You wore your courage on your sleeves as you fought through the turmoil

I owe you, you're the real OG's

You went to war for US on another man's soil. Bringing home that bacon, the poppy seeds, and the oil. When they wanted to end US, you were faithfully loyal. You defended US, you didn't crumble up like foil. You contended for us, my love for you will never recoil. You're the real avenger, the real Mr. Captain America. Thanks for making us independent, for you I tip my cup. With the strength of Thor, you made it possible for US to have the privilege to be free, thanks for standing up. Salute to the Vets, you helped this country live with no limits. You shielded us from threats from enemies and the British. You stopped them from coming and taking over, yes you did it. Revolted the revolution gave US its independence. You gave us the liberty for justice and freedom for all citizens. I write this Will with this Penn to endorse your efforts again Thanks for fighting for our rights you were destined to win. Thanks to all the soldiers R.i.p. to the ones in a potter's field. We would be nothing if it wasn't for your heart and your will You brought US victories. So, it makes sense for me to honor you. Leaving your own family to conquer our enemies was immensely honorable. From the Navy Seals to the Marines, you're my real heroes. They knocked down the towers, but we rebuilt them from ground zero. I hope you continue to be powerful no one can doubt your soul. I hope that you're saluted and appreciated everywhere you go. You deserve respect and honor and credit. Thanks for your service brothers and sisters I'll never forget it

MY MESSAGE TO THE BLACKMAN

Blackman.... When it all goes down, regardless of how you configure it, it isn't respected. You're still considered a nigger in their perspective. It doesn't matter what your nationality or complexion is, you will still get the same reception by their receptionist. To a supremacist your melanin would never be accepted unless it is used for their benefit or businesses. I doubt that you'll be neglected if it's in their interest, kid.

We're undermanned in a war that was planned to wipe us off this planet, knowledge is the first step of understanding this. You're the cream of the crop and are from the essence my brethren, but you were told that you couldn't measure up to their standards of a peasant. That's just all a misconception of a mental perception that they're trying to instill in you to kill you. But never give in to their heckling. For every second that you pay attention to them, you take away from your own self-affection. Then sooner or later, your spirit would be broken and misdirected. But check this, never ever put yourself second again!!! Whether you're Dominican, African, or Mexican, we are all innocent immigrants that are affected by this. I just came to lead you from the Pharisees like Moses did in Exodus. To warn you from the parodies and tragedies of Amerikkka's next of kin. Don't ever be afraid to exceed their measurements. I'm a living testament. I've been tested by them, they tried to down me and not crown me, but I never let it in my mind profoundly when I was contested by them.

I found myself in the mirror, then things started to get clearer, when I put that fear of failure in my rear. huh!!! (Rick Ross voice) I trusted in God to be there when I needed him, he will hear ya and get nearer if you believe in him. I gain mental freedom. You have to have faith in yourself. Blackman, I empathize with your plight. We know it's not right, but if we unite, we could win this fight. You got to invoke your rights to vote and stay awoke. They're like thieves in the night. You'll never see their subtle approach, until their knees are on your throat trying to choke your hopes.

Our protection from this is sticking together so we can end this quick. We can make a difference if we just put aside our indifferences. The epidemic is not a gimmick. They're trying to end us with death sentences that we can't see if we're sleeping with the fishes. They disguised the lies in infections and injections in the Department of Corrections, cold hearted negligence. I hope you're listening.

We are created in God's images. Don't let them devils trick you with their viciousness into thinking we're separated by nationalities, cultures, or religions. Peace, love and unity is my only mission. Which now seems impossible. Whether it's Mexico or Toronto, love has no boundaries, never let them lock up your soul. We got to stop the new Jim Crow laws. Close the doors, because when it reigns, it pours on the rich and the poor. We all wear ponchos eventually. It never made sense to me. we have the same skin color but never acknowledge each other is a mystery. They view us as tyrants. But they're gentrifying our environments. Open your eyelids!!! The time is.... Now! Blackman!!!

Raising Suns

Come on sun stop crying, I'm not trying to replace your dad. But I do gotta thing for your moms my bad, but you ain't gotta be like that. I am not trying to take her from you, that wouldn't be right. I'm just in love with her, hopefully one day she'll be my wife. I know it must be strange when you wake up in the middle of the night and don't see her in your sight. I even try to put up a fight, to get her to go back home to you before the day hits the light. Because I know you need her and don't like it when I am with her, but it's gonna be alright. I know you're probably too young to understand these poems or what I see in her. Maybe when you're grown you'll know what I mean to her, and the spirit and the energy that I breathe in her. So, she can feed you please don't be cruel, I need her too. If I was you, I'd probably hate me too if I was at the other end of the table when I'm needing pastries and food and she wasn't around but there's no need to be rude. My love for her is profound, I'm a good dude.

I know your dad is probably putting me down like I'm a bad guy. But I ain't the one that's beating her and giving her them black eyes, nor am I mistreating her, putting tears and bags under her sad eyes. Please don't fear, come here, don't cry.... you're mad, why? I know we haven't met yet face to face nor do we see eye to eye, but nevertheless I love you just like you were one of mine. You're welcome for them Nike sweats and Jordan number 9's.

I might be the best dad that you have had you'll see in due time. I know it's not your fault that you have a hatred for me in your mind. Of course, that was all your father's thoughts he indirectly designed. He probably thinks that I'm trying to take over his place, but that's not the case. I'm just trying to put a smile on your mom's face, every day and make sure there's food on your plates. Did you say your grace? I could understand the hate, but it's misplaced. That's a big mistake that a lot of fathers make. That guilt, the pride... It's hard to swallow the taste.

But it's okay, that doesn't make him fake or less than great. He's just overprotective, I respect it. He's just trying to keep you and your mother safe. I just want to be a positive motivation and take her out on dates. Maybe one day I can take you to the arcades and let you play all the games if I get the okay, okay? I don't want you to feel uncomfortable when you come home from school expecting him to be there, but if you do I understand because I care. I was like that once too. Here, I got something for you. No, it's nothing to punish you. It's soul food... Something for your soul and your stomach too, I know what you're going through, and only through my poems I can show you. Here, you can have this new ps5 and extra remote controller too, you ain't got to wait until Christmas. I actually grew up fatherless and didn't have many gifts either. So, I get your drift.

But you got plenty, especially in your mother's jewels. Just make sure that you respect and obey her then everything will be cool. If you need help with your homework after school, I got you. Just by me loving your mom,

I'm going to do everything that a father is supposed to do. By the way you could halla at me too, I'm approachable. Whatever you may go through I can guide you and coach you. I'll show you the ropes, so you won't fall for the okie dokes. I promise to be patient, I know that kids can get emotional. I just hope you know that I got your back. I won't leave or fold, just for the simple fact I needed a dad at your age. So, I can understand your rage we're in the same book, I'm just on a different page.

It's going to be okay. I'm going to help you rise and shine every day. Sun, the world is yours, but it's your choice to take.

Black is Black

I can't make this up, even if I tried. You treated me like I was less than. I felt like my heart died. We're the same skin color brother, yeah you and I. I hope that you don't think you're exempted from racism or somehow parted ties. We are all shades of blackness, just a different part of the pie. Even if you attempted to name a difference like a skin blemish or marks around your eyes. We are all black, that's a fact that you can't depart or deny.

Black is Black
Just because you're from the motherland that doesn't mean you can disown US bruh. That doesn't make you any better than me because you came from a different culture. We all have the same sun in the sky and besides soldier, we are all black in their eyes so, can you please control your composure? We have both experienced apartheid once upon a time in our lives. Although we may be divided by a religion hypothesis, you should still empathize. Hopefully we both have the same intentions. Which is love peace and happiness and to be free from the Willie Lynch's lynch men lynchpins that would be magnificent. So don't look at me like we're indifferent.

Black is Black
 No matter what the shade of your skin blend is, that's an artifact fact. The slave masters named US Mexicans, Haitians, Africans, and Dominicans. In reality we are all brothers and sisters no matter how many categories they try to put us in. From the beginning,

from Black Adam and Eve, we're descendants. But somehow in their unjust court systems we became codefendants.

Black is Black

we should be unified, not divided by suits and ties. We all have the same exact black resemblances as the man that was crucified. Yeah....Lucifer lied. How can you turn your back on your race, then look at your face and face the mirror? That is similar to self-hate, interior. Don't let money and power devour your soul and dignity. You may not have any felonies, but you are no different than me. How can you respect the other man more than your own brother man? That's what I can't understand, and by the way, Christopher never even discovered this land!!!

Black is Black

Just because you went to an Ivy League doesn't make you any brighter than me. When you strip away the artificial essentials, then more than likely you will find to see that you are quite like me. On the road to success, we're both liable to be pulled over for DWBs. Don't down me crown me. We all can be Kings and Queens. Let's bridge peace and unity so we can all succeed. I'm not your enemy nor do I pretend to be your friend indeed, but I love you for the sake of the almighty G-O-D and that will never end so let's begin unity with you and me. **Black is Black**

BYRD IN THE AIR

I can't believe that you're gone and you're still not here. Out of nowhere, like thin air you just disappeared. This is so weird because the good ones keep dying. While the shiesty grimy ones appear to keep multiplying. As my mind drifts.... Wondering why the angels took my man and my ace. As I reminisce, I wished that I could've alternated in your place. I would've rather that than to see the tears drip down on your mother's face. I couldn't even hug her at the wake. I nearly broke down when I saw you in your brother's face…don't go wait. I still get that bitter taste in my mouth when I have to say R.i.p. You always wore your heart on your sleeve, you will always be a part of me. You are always going to be forever in my memories. I could never forget you. You came from a different pedigree. When I had those me against the world tendencies, you would always cheer me up with your sincere positive energy. You always kept a smile on your face. I never seen you angry or finicky. You seldom drank. I never even saw you smoke weed.

Maybe with me you would take a sip of Hennessy but when I heard you had cancer, I needed some answers like how can this be? Then when you passed, I was flabbergasted, like God should've taken me. I remember we used to go hard throwing rocks at the penitentiaries. You told me that if I keep bogarting, I will get locked up eventually. You told me that I was too nice and polite, and these streets weren't meant for me. You were right. That was the best advice that you have ever given me. Because I ended up taking heed and it changed my mentality and matured mentally. You were always a stand-up guy, solid as a rock in these streets, when you got popped you never mentioned me. Honor and loyalty were our principles plus we were discreet .No matter what our credentials were we would never deplete or show any type of being weak. I was tripping but I would always listen to your unique critiquing. Because I knew you were spitting the illest wisdom, your expertise was what I needed. You were my brother; I used to love the constructive criticism. Even though you're gone, you will forever live long through your children's children. R.I.P. T-Byrd aka Rich with the positive contagious smile. May you continue to guide me as I try to tame my ways that are wild. I put them drugs down as you would emphatically suggested. My mind is clear now, no longer is it combative or congested. As I try to digest this, it's still hard to stomach your absence. But thanks for blessing me with your greatest gifts which was your smile and your presence. I will never forget it, I'm too heartbroken to shed a tear. Our last words spoken were rare. I love you bro, even though I am wishing and hoping you were here, but I'm going to smile at the good times we had over them years. I know you're in heaven smiling down so here's a spiritual toast for you…. Chea!!!

JUDGE A JUDGE

All that judging that you do is pointless and rude, because when you point the finger, you got three pointing right back at you. To tell you the truth, all the opinions and assumptions you have perused really say something about you and how you move. I live for God, so I ain't got nothing to prove to you... and besides any way who are you? It's not like you got on a black robe or a suit. There's no need to probe into what I do or who I pursue because your opinion is the opposite of overdue, I'm over you. I don't even know you, dude go do you!!!

It seems the most criticism you accrued can come from a person that you vaguely even knew but they're so quick to give a conclusion based on some irrelevant fake news. You shouldn't be so quick to judge or ridicule especially when you don't have the facts or if it's cruel. That's a bad move because we all have flaws at different magnitudes. Divided we fall together we stand as you already knew. A great attitude will have you reaching higher altitudes you can't preach to the choir if you're faulting the pews

You should check yourself before you try to wreck someone else. We all fall short of the glory, but with God things tend to correct themselves. I'm sure we all have regrets that we must live with. No one is perfect, but if you believe with conviction, that's all that really matters; he knows your intentions. You got to let the gossip go right past you and then endow your submission. Even though I may have a couple of screws missing and may not be the sharpest tool in the kitchen, I still take heed and listen. To receive his benedictions, I repented. So, it's crickets to my critics. I'm content because your content is mad malicious.

So, I don't really need your validations. I don't care how you think of me or your evaluation. Luckily only God can ultimately justifiably judge me, therefore your opinions of me don't budge me
Love me!!!

Chapter 6: School's in Su©©e$$ion.

Who am I?

Who am I? A supreme intelligent Blackman with 50 shades of brown on my hand. That's not afraid to take a chance or a stand for any circumstance. Who smiles when adversity comes around because I can defeat any beast and I fear no man. I overstand now that I count!!! and my accounts amount to surmount of me even being black or brown. I'm an overachiever who graduated from the University of Hard Knocks, no cap, or gowns. I'm from blocks where they had to sell rocks in the playgrounds where them kids used to live but because of covid, they can't even play now because of the various contaminated viruses sprayed all over the damn ground.

Who am I? I'm the guy, who never laid down on my town. I stuck to my pledge, when the feds came around cuffed me then tucked me in their beds. With no fair warnings they would swarm in and put thorns to crown my head. They tried to drown me, but instead I read and bled but never feared the ledge. They judged me then put gavel guns to my head then unfairly said "Take these three unsquared meals or 69 rounds full of cold lead" As I beg and pled, Mrs. Amerikkka took my liberty led me away in a sledge, in a cold world they really had me on edge. Threatening me with their hammers cocked and aimed at my third leg. Just in case, I wouldn't be able to procreate the nurtured eggs. They made me thirsty and unfed. In this same injustice sentence this country's grammar is on read. It was hotter than an illicit convicted convict sitting in summer slammer, but words from my grandma encouraged me to flourish so thank God I had her.

Who am I? A King who never squealed a sound when they asked me to snitch on my friends, who are still around because they knew that I was innocent. I will never let them down. I popped off like pills they tried to make it stick. They had cops that would rob us with deals, with stacked decks that weren't slick. but we still posed in jail pics with no visits. They tried to make me ribbit but instead I gave them just crickets. They still put steel in my meals, that inharmoniously made us grit. They played flagrant, like six foul fowls that never got ejected or evicted. How they spun my head like wild owls or dry towels I never accepted it. I was like wow Aww ouch! But I could never bow down or respect it, so I rejected it. They put me in predicaments to get them pigs to split my wig on them 2nd shifts. They put me in cold cells, I was canned like a tuna fish. They greeted me with fists in my armpits or with spit and piss. I did time with chills down my spine and cuffs on my shins and wrist. They polluted me and saluted me with non-Hasidic hazardous languages. The mayor gave us no mayo on them deserted desert dry bologna sandwiches.

Who am I? The same black guy that didn't know why my grandpa died with no wills. I was just a lil bad kid, I had to sleep with no pillow and eat them no frills. The food wasn't as real as the General's meals, but they still gave those bills. The only thrill I would get is when I used to sit at my mother's windowsills at six. I would still steal, dreaming of one day my nightmares will become real. I had to go out there despite the screeches of sweet tooth Uncle Will trying to get me to deal his pills. All he would give me back was a speech that was nil. I had to listen to this hypercritic non-religious Christian that I wanted to kill.

Who am I? The same black child who was raised in a jail cell with the meat fed to me being a mystery. My family couldn't pay the bail, so I had to rot in hell in pity and misery. For four trumped up charges for a sale with reasons unfitting to me. That was just to get me to cop a plea to a felony so I couldn't bear arms evidently, I will never be free!!!

Who am I? I'm the same guy who grew up in an underworld that was a little bit different, who thought the only options were drug dealing and pimping. We communicated with non-enumerated sex drives, just to relieve the stressful emissions. The community got high to get by. We were blessed with these wretched conditions. We all came from broken homes we under slept in and didn't own. They were filled with smoke from cigarettes, butt we were living grown. We had to live reckless in rat infested cribs. Nothing worked, auntie owed Derick and Conned Edison and gave it to whoever came first. We wore the same shirt inside out as we played in the dirt.

Who am I? The same guy who's handsome, Spanish, and fly who understands why they don't want us to unite or comply with the same God in the sky. So, they give us permission for division with a religion from a guy. Every version is different, hopefully the edition is in good intentions, right?

Who am I? That young black boy that you said "no" to. Who would grow into a blind rage, with pain in his eyes that you can't see because it's hidden behind his shades. My heart is hollow; my eyes are sleepy from the task force forcing a raid. Trying to divide my family, I had to swallow my pride at the cost of my age.

Who am I? That same boy who used to post up in the corner stores to corner whores for quarts of milk. I knew all the guilt that was filled in their drawers, but they spoiled me still. They did strange thangs for change, but they had to pay bills or remain poor. It rains on the wealthy and the unhealthy whether I chill, it's the same pour. Being broke is a joke so pay attention that's not a coincidental metaphor. There's no hope in dope or a successful potential I never met before.

Who am I? A guy who learns from his mistakes, who can take wine and turn them into grapes. I never whined or cried behind those gates while I learned how to wait. Although I never got caught, my freedom was still steal taken at eight. They raised the stakes, then adjourned the courts until I was 28. They sold my social security in stocks in sections of quarters and eights. Luckily, I prayed to Allah and had a positive mind state that would never fluctuate. I don't know how many times I been upstate for a sale that I didn't make, but it doesn't make me any less than great. Such as LeBron or Mary J. Sometimes I just wanted to go hug my mom's but couldn't but knew it would be ok. I'm just one of the millions the yanks help freed as slaves. Like Doc Gooden but it shouldn't have had to be that way. They said I couldn't, but I could if I was to see it that way.

Who am I? I'm just a guy that's trying to take my mistakes and make good of it. Hopefully create a place so others less fortunate in the hood could inherit. I want to teach adolescents, so they don't have to make the same regressions. Without having to go through what I went thru to learn that lesson. I'm hoping that they can take heed and use these seeds and earn a blessing. It's my open secret way of giving back to God, showing my progressions. I survived plandemics, recession, depressions, getting tested and corrected. As a man I never ran from a clan or couldn't ever plan this testament. It was just meant to happen, no capping, that accident was a measurement. It all falls in God's plans and actions. The additions and the subtractions. I came from the ashes and regained my happiness. I couldn't have imagined this. I hope the youth refrain from gangs and the vicious madness of attractions and get ready to set goals. I did the time for you already, so you don't have to trip or strip away your pride, slow your role.

Who am I? I'm just that black guy with 5 felonies trying to excel in these streets. Trying to achieve what the haters and naysayer's telling me that I can't be. I'm just a show that won't ever get canceled unless God permits it to be. Because the almighty Allah got a plan for you, and he sent it through me. Don't ever listen to them that tells you what you can't do or can't be. God wouldn't give you nothing that you couldn't handle, so breathe. You're fabulous, and it's never too late to chase your dreams. Like Meek Mill, you can start out with a nick and let it stream. Fate seems to have a different time span than Iran or Japan, you will see. Time went to iPhones from a wristband then switched hands in a God week. So, you can if you think you can, Ali and Eve. You just have to believe and follow your dreams.

Who am I? That's a good question that you're asking me, but I have too many personalities that I keep forgetting. As for me I just do my best impression of what I think God asks of me. Without regretting it, so I can pass my heeds to my seeds after me.

WAKE UP!!!

Wake up wake up wake up wake up!!!
When are you going to wake up?
Hopefully, not in slavery handcuffs.
When are you going to open your eyes?
When you see yourself in a demise?
Don't you already see, all that they have ruined?
What about your family tree, what are you doing?
Where's your focus? It's sure not on the prize!
Only the wise will see through the uncivilized.
But if you're getting too high or sleeping all day.
How can you, in real life, realize and separate the real from the fake?
Or the truth from the lies in real-life as it is being displayed?
They're tricking you constantly on tell-lie-vision aka Tv.
That sly Fox is only putting on what they want you to see.
The revolution or the solution will never be televised. Take it from me.
It's easy like a-b-c and 1-2-3 basically.
It's really simple but you can't hear or see.
Because you got too many issues going into your temples evidently.
They're only chopping, screwing, and redoing HIStory.
It's more to it than meets the eyes.
They're transforming like Optimus prime.
Right In front of your face.
What you think you see on your optimum or prime
Is just a reflection, it's front and a fake.
Big Brother has been watching you the whole time.
Through the sky with clear reception.
But you're so hella high that you keep on forgetting.
Now they got the tv's watching you on the flipside.
Even through the Echoes in your kitchen.
You got to choose.... Which side?
You can't play the fences.... that's a thin line.
It's like Brady on 4th and inches against Giant defenses.
That's a winless decision.
I know I'm not going to make any sense
to the unawaken or the blind.
They don't seem to be interested in their own interests or of the time.

So, I get it, I won't waste my time... that would be centsle$$
Like trying to count my race on a census.
What does the color of my face have to do with where I'm living?
The only way we overcome hate is with action, love, and repentance.
I'll probably be a nuisance to those choosing to be illiterate.
Or the unwise student whose mind isn't open to receive wisdom gifts.
From the words that I have spoken.... I know this isn't a myth.
My 2cents would be useless to students who aren't prudent.
Or ones whose spirits are broken or don't want to listen to my music.
I'm going to let that soak in, hoping you don't get lost in confusion.
Wake up wake up wake up wake up!!!
I can't force you to drink water from a fountain of knowledge
but I hope you see the wisdom and understand it when you find it.
Dear youth, I can only share the truth in these poetry seeds.
That I hope you read, and it leads to you bearing fruit voraciously.
I only strive to teach you from the slaughters and tortures I bereaved.
Through my devotions as a poet, I can show it but can't make you see.
I'm only hoping to open your eyes in hopes you take me gracefully.
A change will happen with actions, you just have to wait patiently.
I hope you'll internalize what I say before it's your turn, listen to me!
Because we all must see that dreaded judgement day eventually.
I just want you to know that it's ok to make a mistake, but don't quit.
Apply yourself, it won't be easy, you're great, you're equipped.
It will only make you smarter and go harder my brethren.
Because that's all part of.... The process is called progression.
Wake up wake up wake up wake up!!!
To be aware is to be alive.
Once you know, you shouldn't repeat the same mistakes in life.
Doing something that doesn't work over and over again,
expecting different results is insane, no one is exempt.
In order for them to take US more seriously we must be efficient.
In our protesting. We must be specific and be prolific.
Wake up wake up wake up wake up!!!

Wake up niggas!!!

They say the vaccination is the new assassination and a way for racist businesses to enforce Jim Crow laws on blacks and Asians. While the deathacrats and the redumbagains get a placebo. For population control, they already have full fledged plans of replacing you. Now, when you're given the poisonous poke, you get a passport. The news is confusing and brainwashing my folks to become an afterthought. Now in half the sports, you can't even enter their arenas without that jab. They want to see the proof or see the magnetic scab, yea it's that bad. You can't even get a pass for religious purposes. Antichrists and communists don't care who you worship. They fear unity and anti-subordinates. They're scared; they're pro willie Lynch and pro black abortionists. Using us against us to kill us off quick. Our mind is in the clouds. Killing a child before they even get a chance to smile is wild. Even before they even get a chance, they're throwing in their towel in advance. Though they are certain legit circumstances. The government is like Mickey D'z they're loving it, killing kids like China did but doing it in the stomachs. They don't want US to grow up to be an activist or a scientist, fearing retribution dreading they would get severe punishment. Meanwhile prison is slavery revisited. They are closing down the state jails just to overcrowd the Federal system and you can't go against them, their defense funds are unlimited.

Giving middlemen jail time that's infinite, unless they infiltrated illegal Rico businesses, meaning to snitch on them. They're literally arresting our development because of our melanin. They try to label US felons and/or rebellions, so we can't vote then disable our rights to bear arms amendment. It's hard to cope with this predicament. I'm sick and tired of being broke and defenseless. The constitution is only for Amerikkka. Their laws restrict us because they're scared of us, they really try to constrict us by convicting us, then convincing us that we are bugged. They supplied the inner urban cities with guns and drugs, then they locked up "El Chapo" for show, but the government was the socket to the plug. They aided and abetted to let it flood the streets like Ida tho, I don't know a dealer that can grow his own control substances, that's psycho bro. They will let us kill each other but if your real with your brother, the Feds will put so much time over your head it'll make a quitter squeal on his mother. The black ghetto is still filled with racist cops that are instilled with hate that you may get shot when they raise their Glocks. Wake up wake up wake up you better wake up niggers!!! The gaming stops!!!

STAY AWAKE!!!

Soon as they complete the covid19 vaccines. The opps is going to drop the covid 2020s on the scene. Stay awoke in this PLANdemic. Stack your money in a safe. Stay safe. Protest in other ways, they're coming for your waist. Marching is just making you more vulnerable for their attacks. Don't be their test dummies. Depart from the packs. Start your own business, invest your time into family and fitness. We got to start from scratch and make plans that's definitive. This isn't just a coincidence. This has been written since the days of Nostradamus. It's about to get ugly, prepare to defend against their violence. Don't be silent. Trump and his supporters are already trying to sabotage and torture us with their new world orders, bruh. Trying to enforce abortive laws on your daughter, while our sons are in these streets getting slaughtered. They imported divide and conquer tactics, while we at home relaxing. Don't get caught up, we are under attack kid!!! Never let that fact be left on your mattress or you'll wake up in slavery, without your worldly attachments. While we're out here being the flyest and the highest, they're being the modest and dishonest planning ways for our demises.
Wake up Wake up Wake up!!! Open your eye lids!!!

Realize Real Lies

We need to support each other instead of aborting each other, there's too much division. If it's not one thing then it's another, there's too much disgruntling bickering. Even in the households that we are living in. There are sisters against brothers and fathers against mothers, it's sickening. The black family is in collision and subsidized for grim incentives. They're making less homes for the homeless to be sheltered in big percentages. Nowadays people will respect racist dead presidents, more than their own family they're coexisting with is evident. We are poor choice forced to live in a pest infested residence. That can actually have an aftereffect on our mental conceptions. I hate to see someone in need ask for help and felt like a peasant, and their own people are so selfishly feeling themself that they're hesitant. But the same people, be so quick to buy foolery to be fluorescent, or designer clothes and overpriced Nike's to feel loved and accepted. This new generation is filled with hateration, clout chasing and crabs in the bucket mentality infectionations. If you were to give them positive advice, they would only look at you like you are crazy and not be receptive to what you're saying. Meanwhile they'll hype the radio stations filled with songs of prostitution promotion professes, drug using, and shootings, butt that's all being respected??? I'm not trying to down you, I'm just striving to crown you with these dialectics, like the kings and queens that I see in you, if only you don't reject it. Like you did Huey P, Ella Josephine Baker, and Malcolm X's rhetoric. They were all killed in the line of fire to stop their righteous messages. So, how can you trust the government successors' successions, when they're the one who kidnapped our forefathers then placed them in prison systems like they were domestic terrorists? Their plans are to have us out of sight and out of mind. Steven could even see the genocides and he's blind. For instance, do you ever sit and think then wonder why the minorities make up the majority in the prisons that they occupy? Do you think that this is just a big coincidence or that Amerikkka targets our men and children to fill up their big prison businesses? Is it so that our women are to have no guidance or respect for their men, or our protection from the devil's deception that they're in? Or is it that their intentions are is to have our women turn to other races or to other women, and to look at us as an opposition and need replacements in these circulating events? Or is it that their Willie Lynch mission is for our kids to grow up with no directions to be raised by electric gadgets and televisions to have them subjected to these abrasive directive's tactics. Exposing them to gangs and drugs in the environment that they are living in. Or maybe this is just one of my deranged envisionings.... How many more of us got to die, for you to see the real from the lies is the question that I'm asking for you to self-conceptualize? Do you realize what the enemy is trying to do? Does it actually have to happen to you, for you to take considerable actions of pursuit? I am not lying to you. The truth is plain to see in real life. Does it have to be your own family for you to see the calamity with your own congealed eyes? Or does it have to be your own daughter that gets kidnapped and tortured for body parts, in order for you to realize that your temple is a body art that God created that was properly formed. Or does it have to be your own son that the system takes away in their freights, and he's mentally and physically raped for you to see the light??? Does it really have to get that real for you to stand up and fight this unrighteousness? I hope you open your third eye and soak in these pious hymns. There's a war going on outside and they're mobbing deep, so don't sleep. They're causing havoc on our prodigies. It's hell on earth in our society. Knowledge is a tree, find a leaf.

SOULS4SALE

It's crazy how they will buy your votes and endorsements with invisible money gimmicks. Don't be crying when they force those poisonous vaccines when the PLANdemic finishes. Then they will try to instill new world-order chips they want to exist in your wrist, but y'all not wise or seasoned to believe it until you see it diminishing. Cold facts... You're still black! Whether you're Mexican, Puerto Rican or Dominican. We all have been victimized by systemic racism or patriotic paganism. All I can do is my poetic mission envisaged for my brothers and sister's spirits, but I hope y'all praying for wisdom because they're preying and are very vicious. The road to hell is paved with good intentions. Our vote was just a debatable debacle, if you really were listening. All you had to do was pay attention to what their body language was mentioning, and how they refused to answer the vital viral questions that were specific. You could have made your decision then, because you have just witnessed it. They're buying elections now, so how can we overcome oppression or defeat these supremacists?

ARISE AND FLY

They will try to use and abuse you, then when you want to know something, they will try to confuse you. They will start arguments between friends then act neutral. Then use reverse psychology, having you in the deep end of a stagnant pool. The power is shifting in Amerikkka, you better know the rules. The ones who have their monetary numeric up will perish you, they are so cruel. No Jimmy Choo, you can't step in my shoes. I walk my own path. I move how I move my respect is due. We are all unique, we don't have to compete. We can all have the riches and businesses while living in peace. But it's obvious that the Naviance is not complete. They're trying to kill us either physically and mentally, capeesh. But possibly we can achieve in these streets as scholars and not be just another one collared like the greens that we seek. Why is it daily that I see, black men getting shot by the police? And rarely do we ever receive any type of relief? Why do I care or bother? Because I gotta, sheesh! That could've been you or me. The means is beseeched for us not to believe. We are watching too much tv while the opps is on the creep trying to rock us to sleep timelessly, just ask Philippe. But you don't see the cross at night because you're too busy with your cellphone lost in their sights, meanwhile they're raising hell in your home. What's in those wells is unknown. They trail us with drones, the beef is fake, you couldn't tell it was cloned??? They're mixing cow tongue with chitlins and grinding, it stay grounded, cook your own

. I shouldn't have to repeatedly remind you of this when it is shown. Let's stop the snickering and the bickering, let's unite, we're grown. They substituted jails from our thrones and withheld the chromes. They disqualified us with felonies at 17 years old, but we were too young to know, because we were getting stoned. That was all part of their plans to somehow unarm US as a man. They look at us as targets. Why can't we just all get along in this land? It's a shame, but we may never reach financial independence, because we don't even invest substantial support in our own businesses. You must invest your wealth in your health like a gymnast. Make that cash you flip naturally without having to depend on a chemist. We are too quick to reinvent some irrational ways of thinking. We are too worried about fashions or stuck in a relationship that is quickly sinking. All we're worried about is hoes, polos, and the newest sneakers. My Jewish features have them like "yo, you're too cheap sun" Nah I'm just fugal, if you only knew, you'll be too. Invest and keep something and don't be neutral with your money like a dummy, because they will take from you and from me, then distribute it back to another country. Meanwhile in Africa there are people still hungry, and that's the richest continent. All the most valuable resources come from there, raise your consciousness. Especially when your dollars don't make any kind of sense. It's worthless to be living paycheck to paycheck, spending mortgage-like money just to pay your rent. You ain't got a pot to piss in or a window to throw it in, but your outfit is splendid and you're living in contentment? Gentrification is real. Their dedication to dead our nation is instilled deep in their roots. But Since Emmett Till, y'all timid still. Do you need any more proof? They're lying on seals, we're lying still. We rather chase cake, women, and thrills until our toes are cut off and we got to foot the bills. Then we wonder why our kids is feminine and unreal, because they are raised by single mothers who bash their child's father while he's on them pills. Or in the streets or jail, with all this self-defeat on repeat we are doomed to fail. They tried to confine us to private prisons to divide us from our kids and beautiful women. *America*: which side do you live in? With devilish vicious intentions they're coming at our mankind in ways that's efficient and different, and sublime but we're blinded. Not to mention......the drugs.... the lies .... The tell-lie-visions. My peoples are too high to envision the visions that Malcolm X was mentioning. What if Rosa parks never sat on them back benches? I ain't finished. You rather turn your cheek than be an eyewitness. (R.I.P. Junior) Another black kid murdered in these streets is ridiculous and weak. This time it wasn't by the police.... sheesh!!!! This black-on-black killings has to cease. Facts, PEACE. It's so strange that all we know is rap, sex, drugs, and gangs. All we do is make memes and complain about the pain. It seems like these marches and speeches isn't doing anything. It's not giving US gains. It seems like the Freedom Liberty bell never rang. In them heavy dark clouds, there isn't too much rain, just information on how to keep us uninformed and tamed. The 5g nuclear and coronavirus synonymously were designed to give us pain. Seeing, but not doing anything is like living in vain. Through the kaleidoscopes we collide with hope and disdain. Putting dope in our veins trying to cope with pain. I know I'm insane because I sure did the same... When I was younger trying to feed my siblings hunger pains to maintain. Where I come from, the poverty rate is a shame. They are dying dumb young not using their brains, infused with the haze. They are just trying to get by, getting high, confused in this maze. Getting entrapped in the trap, perusals of the game. Stop frying your lungs before you die sun. From the stress, cigarettes in your flesh is an intensive death you're causing yourself.

You don't get it yet??? Is it because you are too high to apply the wisdom and intellect, to understand the visions that's within your concepts? The ability is in you, not Tom cruise to get the mission accomplished. Arise and fly the sky is the limit only you is stopping you,

So stop it

175

PICK YA POISON

Whether the President is Trump or Biden, being efficient is the only way for US to benefit from the politics they are providing. We must start electing God first and incorporate our own businesses. I'm just being earnestly honest and telling it how I witnessed it. This plandimic's silver lining has given us the opportunity to think outside the boxes, and for us to take off and FLY and be pilots. They must feel like it's a privilege for us to be living but don't trip. God has higher mileages than any SUV, jet, or ships. So, if you can survive this ridiculous 2020's there's no limit to what you can achieve. Let it be the vision that you can see, all the hypocrisies and the political fallacies. I got on my knees and thanked God for every morning that I opened my eyes and see,

it's another chance for me to succeed no matter what the weather be or who wins this presidency. Because where I live, in poverty-stricken NYC the gentrification is increasing but decreasing our population yes indeed. If we don't have a plan in the making, we will be left naked in these streets. That's just my observation that I see in this demon democracy. It's time for US to start applying pressure to Amerikkka obviously. We won't vote but we'll stand in line for the lottery. Way before there was a "black vote" there were laws to not have blacks vote. Jim Crow laws caused massive hysteria to black folks. So how can they use that approach when they want to campaign? How dare US, be oblivious to their conniving ways this has got to change. You can see it like night and day. They don't even put shades on their lying ways. Their lies are bright, right in your face. They're strident and don't even deny or justify it but give us just the lies quick. This is not rocket science. The corruption in justice lies within its systematic ways to control, hold, and mold to keep a Blackman a slave. Too many bad acts have happened, they're never going to change. Even though I know we can't turn back the page, there's no need for rage. We must show action to let them know that we are not playing. All these politics are just lies, polished with cliché sayings. Because it seems like every day I wake up and watch the news I see another

Blackman getting shot or tased, I'm confused. Seeing a tot popped by a cop with a Glock issued to a racist is the issue that I'm facing today. It's the same ish since 86. Amerikkka's back to its blatant ways. The white supremacists don't want you to hear this, so they might take this away. They use attractions and distractions or other tactical ways. They will assassinate our character and embarrass us in practical ways. They call us terrorists and tyrants when all we want is peace and the police to stop the violence. All we want is their brutality to cease, sheesh!!! Not too much has changed since back in the days. They are still killing us and not getting properly charged, butt the stimulus will make it all go away. They'll call up the National Guard to violate our freedom of speech. That is beyond my reach of understanding we need more pieces to see peace. None of these presidents has been a resident of a shelter but they claim to change homelessness to show support and help us. It sounds like sodium from that pedestal podium. When they get into office they won't deal with the boondocks, Nickelodeon. It's just another Bob with square pants trying to square dance on our issues. But when it comes down to getting to you, they will continue to miss you. They will issue more help to other countries overseas than to help home right here, where we have a war on poverty. So, when you pick your poison pick the one with less venom. Just make sure your intentions are protecting our children and our women

. I'm tired of asking for budgets and equality. For that we can see that they're not budging when it comes to our needs. Unless it's for their benefits we must put an end to this and force them to reap the repercussions from their racial injustices. The republicans and democrats are puppets of the government. We must make our votes count and valid for them to candidly function. Whatever way you have it, the challenge is to pick the lesser poison in the ballots. That is in conjunction with demanding results and production. The red or blue pill consumption is still hard to stomach. But we must make them do something. Make sure you do the math and don't go by assumptions. They will always conceal their intentions when they're on your television pulpitting for a position in any political junction. It won't be that obvious and the only way to stop their dumbness and dominance and for our issues to be prominent, is by choosing a side with the lesser corruption. Pick your poison… but make sure that your decision is picked with precision. So, your votes count when they count the votes. Just don't stand there and do nothing to show your position.

Pick ya poison.

DO BLACK LIVES STILL MATTER?

Word to Big pun we will overcome this dumbness, I mean Trump/pence the angels will soon blow their trumpets. They're backed by hatred and racism in front of our faces. This is Amerikkka, the home of the fashionist fascism. What are you really trying to make great again? I don't know what to make of this. They became so blatant. Paganism, not even Ronald Reagan was this flagrant, or evasive and this is an abomination to our nation. We are Obama's nation.

They're trying to leave us all naked running around homeless and brainless. Why are all our so-called leaders remaining nameless? We all got the same 24 hours without Jack Bauer. Our power is in our dollars, but we're stuck on name brands on our collars. If we spend our proceeds back on our own seeds we can succeed in reviving Black Wall Street. We're too cheap, when it comes to black owned businesses. We're way too concerned about what he or she did to get it. Instead of coming together and having a collective bargaining, we live fake lavish lives and accept this uncorrected marshaling. We will still shop at the Walmart's 'n' Target's and pay rent to a laconic Masonic owner, mortgages and live in cribs that have forfeitures. It's ironic, we put blood diamonds on chains and tints on whips. Then fund white supremacist's businesses so they can enrich their kids. They say "all life matters" to counter protest our mission.

All lives aren't taken by crooked cops or given long sentences. The unfair disparities in the corrupted justice system. Is apparently creating a better living for them. So stop it Karen and Kevin, you can spare me with that. Like you have the same struggles compared to being black.

Or a minority or whatever way they wanna put us in a category. It's 2020's we're still dealing with racism? That's a sad story. Black Lives Matter, let's stop going backwards my brethren. Slow progress is better than no progress, keep stepping.

REAL E$TATE

Respectfully, I just seen $um Jews in my hood in front of a house for sale. Gentrification is real and you don't have to travel to Jerusalem to see what I feel. But you won't see if you're in a cell. Whether it's in a prison or your mind is mentally in a jail. But I'm going to school you before they fool you, without you having to go through Yale. These are just tales from the hood that I tell. Yeah, it's scary, I hope you awake from sleeping on yourself. We all have the same hours and the powers but it's how you utilize your wealth. The timetables will tell on how your able to be stable like a shelf, to stand on your own two after you fell invest in your health!!! That in turn will yield more kale than a million cents on a scale and make a lot of sense. I meant to hope you can feel me like Braille. I'm off this I have new ships to sail. But I hope y'all pay attention to the new apartments for sale.

Wake up Everybody

The Sun won't shine forever. No matter what the devils try to endeavor, we got to stick together. GODS on earth isn't nothing new however, if you knew better, you'll do meta better. Zeus wasn't as real as you learnt in Greek mythology, the schools fooled you instead of the truth they used tricknology. But the ology is the same psychology, the kkk and illuminati is using the willie lynch scientology to demolish our creed. Now they go through technology to attack our seeds, zap their attention with "tell lies to your visions" aka TV's. The Covid apologies the government for trying to bribe US with its old. The stimulus benefit you get to make you forget, is backed by what gold? That can only grow into an inflation what we are now facing, but that doesn't affect the rich faces and their pecking order placements. Isn't that so strange what they are doing??? This goes back to Africa; they're still laughing at US HUEMANs. But it's not funny, the 5G radiation is causing hysteria. They're silent about the Chinavirus; they let it come to America. It all goes back to knowledge... bruh!!! We're all Asiatic in traffic no matter what the devils try to distract us with... duh!!! No homer. This is way different than the predictions and implements that they're systemin in the Simpsons. Pulp OJ in my juices4life, with real roots like ginseng and garlic in my milk from brown rice. The modern-day slavery lynching is going on in cyclones, while we are getting high off legal weed and stuck on our cell phones. Having US panicking, it's time for Us to be a man again and not a mannequin you need to man up, kid. Understand this quick. They are trying to kill Us! Why would I leave my home of the brave, to come back just to have them claiming that my home is their home, that's insane!

All Allah is doing is bringing US back to remembering him in our brains. Because we got distracted by their attraction of monetary gains. If you pray and have faith, then use that same energy of fear and redirect it to positivity for your peers. Change your ways and put that synergy into God, and then let the psalms lead your day. No weapon formed against you shall prosper as King David says. We're chosen, golden and have the will to live life to the fullest. Just open the presents, Allah gave to you at Christmas. That's every day if you get it. Not as the pagans might depict it. It isn't about just giving gifts. Trust and believe young G, you can conquer any greed. No matter whether you're from Yonkers or NYC. If you're ready you don't have to get ready word to Bun B. I done C the D-Evils F--ing up our economy. All the real OGs are on drugs or locked up in the beast. They fell victim to trapping, going ham for that cheese. No ratting. Reagan's "war on drugs" in the streets, was created to eliminate our race physically and mentally. I have seen this coming way before trump's dumbness. But when Allah's angels blow those trumpets, so goes trump and pence. You can feel it in the air, just as Beanie Siegel learnt it. Allah is greater than any amount of money that they can come up with. Don't be a dummy and fall for the okie dokie tricks. Wake to be great cut your grass and you will see the snakes in the midst. The fake frenemies that will scheme and perpetrate, Wake up!!! Wake up!!! Wake up!!!

…. Before it's too late.

HUEMAN

How can I ever be a racist. We all came into this world naked. Even though my hue might be painted a different shade from you which is true I'm still sainted. I feel the rage and the hatred, but now it's more blatant. Why!!! All our blood is blue when it's veining. It only turns red when it hits the air, it's the same with them. Then why do we live in despair, in-vain and in sin. Or acting inhumane towards other races, one day we will all have to face HIM. The only race that counts is the human race, and it's that basic. So you can hate until you turn blue in the face, or you can just face it. Why would I judge another brother because of his skin color? That's hating!!! There's no toleration for discrimination in this nation.

Mlk had a dream, now that it seems we're awakened and looking for love, peace, and happiness and a place to feel good in. Though I live in the US I could never call myself a citizen. But I do have love for the illiterates, maybe one day they will get it.

We are all immigrants, whether or not you think you know the difference. Even though our involuntary migration might've been different. They said Christopher Columbus only allegedly discovered it, then stripped Miss America after she was raped and pimped. This land that was already here, HIS-story was flipped with tricks. They tried teaching US that, in school to keep us fooled but now I'm hipped. Do the knowledge then you would overstand the gist. I come from a man that descended from the image of Him. Like Jesus's bronze hands from the palms of Allah's fingertips. I hope you know who you are, and you will never forget this. I'm not a racist.

I'm just a hueman that's been targeted by them. But I don't fret I'm armed by God
who gives me strength, wisdom, and beauty. I overstand what they are trying to do to me so I won't slip. I pray that you embrace your hue and live life to the fullest. We all have different hues and different views and influences, but the same sun, earth, and moon to live in harmony like grits. I'm just a super hueman without the cape that goes against, the white supremacists, because that's my duty as a living Hueman activist.

Coco B-aware

How is construction considered essential? They're building them gentrified buildings right before our eyes. This isn't coincidental. That's why they want us inside at night. Did you get the memo? They make it so we can't see their planning of the unbiblical, and the genocides while their masking their credentials. While they're putting the venom outside that goes into your nostril ventricles. Strategical moves, but I know what they are trying to do. I'm already hip to the cold war tactics. This isn't too political. This has been happening since the days of their master Yakub, and their planned disaster, FEMA camp crystal. They're trying to make us sickos to weaken the coco population. Then this nation tried to stimulate us with stimulus sensations. They think the hush money is some sort of compensation. Meanwhile our strong black men and women are in prison and their only release date is masturbation. Our women are with other women and imitating Asians. Our men are with men or trying to be women, self-unassisted emasculating. We're distracted by ratchet TV, chasing chips with closed eyelids not wise pun intended. I hope you don't get offended, but this is where I'm living in. It is what it is, it isn't what it isn't. The government is vicious, consistently malicious with intentions. But we can't fold under pressure or tweak like a weak spine. God said, "no weapon can prosper against any children of mine.

" If you believe that you can do it, then you will be fine. Allah is the guiding light that can lead the deaf and the blind. Prayer with work work and it will outshine any wealth. First and foremost, believing in yourself all the time will help. We must make conscious decisions to be aware of being alive. TV's are full of pollution. The revolution resolution will never be televised. You can't see through the bull whips or get by if you're too high. Open your eyes and stay awake in these last days and times. They aren't playing this time. They're taking names and taking lives. Life isn't a game, ain't no lame going to play with mines. Jan. 6 riot marked the day the beast came out from being quiet. They showed US that we will get nowhere protesting nonviolent. They tried to get the lawmakers to take the bills and re-sign them. The potus incited the riot and still didn't resign. The republican's show US that them and racism are synchronous. Also, synonymous with guilty until proven innocent admonishing them. It left me speechless to see him for the 2nd time beat impeachment. The blatant use of fighting words he twisted and tweaked them. To say that he was just exercising his freedom of speech is blasphemy. To be aware is to be alive I hope you're understanding me, first you must save yourself then go save your family

Adolescent Lessons

When you look in the mirror what do you see? Do you see a young adolescent in the image of G-O-D. Or do you see a nigga with an attitude who likes to smoke weed and watch tv. Or do you see an entrepreneur that wants more than a j-o-b? Whichever way you put ice cubes in your iced tea, just know that you have the free will to choose how you view your ideology. Honestly, I can never pity a fool like Mr. T. Just because you don't see jewels around my neck doesn't mean, I don't bling. I shine differently. I'm enriched with knowledge and choose to spend my checks efficiently without going to college. I was brought up in a hard knock school that taught me how to be frugal effectively. I'm far from cheap. I just couldn't breathe with slave chains around my neck personally, and the only thing worse than greed is envy, curse fully. That just didn't work for me, it only attracted the wrong attention and women with gold digging intentions seeing their worth in me. I knew God had a different purpose for me. I'm just striving to teach the kids, before they see a bid and be in a jail cell like Hellrell and Juelz. Because they won't get that diplomatic immunity when they come home with a felony in their community, I know that story so well. I'm just telling you the truth, myute from my own experiences as I beseech you. These streets are cruel and a cesspool. I am not trying to preach, but I have nephews and a niece that needs my guidance, so I provide it through my actions and what I speak. That time I spent hustling in the streets was worthless to me, because eventually you'll get caught and hauled off to a court then sent to the belly of the beast. Working for pennies, aka modern-day slavery. Sulked and broken with not enough cheese to purchase what was once free. Some chose to turn their backs and rat on their own family but that isn't the man that I be. Free your dome now, those lawyer fees are expensive. The prison system business is full of brownskin men with good intentions, but most just chose bad ways to get out their predicaments. The disparity is conspicuously ridiculous, and you don't want to be a 40year old reminiscing of what you could've did, kid. Get these benefits from my personal experiences quick!!! You got the chance to advance out the hood again and make something good of it. You can learn from my burns and turn from the self-destructive paths and choose better ways to earn your cash like I should've. You only get one life to live. We all make mistakes, but you got what it takes to turn your life around and be something great. You can be a lawyer, a teacher, or a business owner. Or you can go to college for 4years and get yourself a diploma. You now have the opportunities that you need to succeed, and your dreams can be achieved all you got to do is believe!!!

Bad news

It never fails… Every day that I wake up there's nothing but bad news on the news and my subconscious shouldn't really take in this stuff. I can't make this up. Every day another soul is being taken up to the most high like smoke in the sky. As NBC, ABC, sly FOX, and CNN give their reviews without posting why. So, what's a nigga to do when he's bitter and confused. We go from seeing smart kids emptying clips in schools, then seeing reverends pimping out their pews. Then we turn to channel 22 only to overview that our hoods are still messed up. Instead of building them up, all they worried about is earmarks, pork barrows and infrastructures. Which all are to make US to think that they're trying to help our communities, but in reality, they're legally loansharking and money laundering with democratic immunity. The news is also a tool for the government. Yeah, they're loving it, but this isn't Mickey D's. You won't see the subtle settlements in their regiments, they value mils differently. They're conspicuously building commercial buildings right up under us. But they got our vision tunneling, meanwhile they're indirectly turning our kings into queens because that's what they see on the radio and on their TV's. Curiosity got them wondering. Every day they are showing a new conspiracy theory. They made various variants to push those vaccines clearly. Meanwhile Pfizer, Johnson & Johnson and Billy Gates are stacking up that cheese. We are getting attacked in these streets so much that somebody must be handing out them gats for free, so we won't be free, but that's hushed...

shush up! Every day I see murdered blacks on TV. What happened in D.C. would never have happened in N.C. without black casualties. There's no peace, and police are still shooting black teens and capping through their teeth. It's no accident the stock markets are crashing through the breach. But what you won't see is when they free their rioters, and ever since the unemployment and stimulus the streets have been quieter. They legalized weed to enable US to get higher, and how can they pardon the time I did in 95, but it seems like it's too good to be true, especially if it's seen on the news and it's advising you with lies that sound really true. They televised the looting, so the cops could start the shooting. The news is just an illusion of monumental pollution and mental prostitution, but it's all undercover. Every day I discover a new crime when I turn on channel 9 at news time with my brother. If it's not one thing it's the other. Today a brutal bar beating started with a car overheating, and the suspect suspecting the bar owner of cheating. Maybe she was because of his mistreating and misleading her, but when he saw her hugging and kissing Steven, he gave her a reason to get even. Even though he didn't mean it, because he was high. Then I turned to channel 5 to see two teens get shot in the Stuy, one in the leg, one in the eye, both were drive-by's. All the cops recovered was burnt rubber and bullet shells. Witnesses wouldn't tell what they saw like it was some type of rebellion against the police and the law. But that could've been my little niece or my nephew. I know we got a code of the streets but sheesh, respect the youth. Then I turned to channel 11 to see that a 42yr old granddad was stabbed four times in his abdomen on 149th and Madison in broad daylight. These cats ain't playing right in this game of life, say goodnight. Then right at Washington square park, sparks sparked a stampede. I was told the victim was steamrolled like damped weed, amid the chaotic scramble ninjas on banshees was screaming like chimpanzees, that's that damned leak. Then on channel 3 across town on west 137th street, a domestic violence dispute led to a weapon being used and the victim was transported to the hospital. Then they also tried to deface George Floyd's tribute, you know why and who. Motivated by the fuel that the bad news views contributed to. Then I turned to the local news and I almost cried, when I heard that the Yonkers late great Goat, Dmx died... why???? Then at six o'clock a car jacker crashed and hit two tots, then ran past a red traffic light running from the cops then he smashed into that new fast-food spot. Live reporting the bad news for all our people to view, to instill fear all year to be subdued. Through your eyes and your ears, watch what you let appear to tell your vision. Because negativity attracts negativity so pay attention or pay the consequences. They're preying on your consciousness. Watch what you watch at six

More books written or published by Coolgmack
You can order them amazon.com search for coolgmack
I also accept cash apps $coolgmack Or send $20 plus $5 for shipping and handling
with your info/id number to

Coolgmack@gmail.com

Make sure your info like name and institution is clear
You can check out these other books by coolgmack

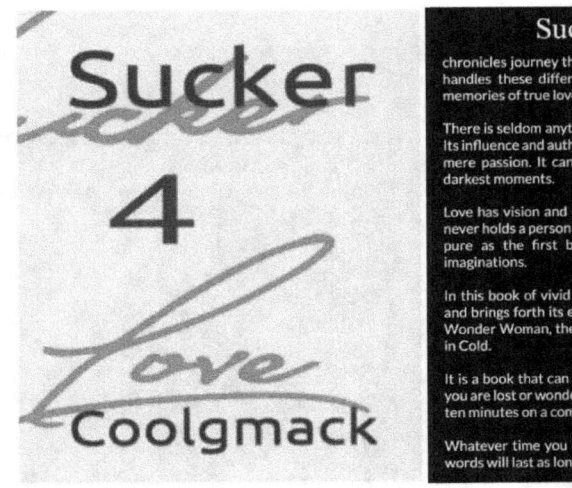

Sucker For Love

chronicles journey through love and heartbreaks and how he handles these different episodes. It also paints beautiful memories of true love and shares hope with enduring in love.

There is seldom anything more powerful or potent than Love. Its influence and authority is greater than hate and better than mere passion. It can heal the gravest wounds and light the darkest moments.

Love has vision and clarity and a purpose all of its own, that never holds a person back and never casts a jealous eye. It is as pure as the first breath we take and as limitless as our imaginations.

In this book of vivid poetry, Love is examined in all its finery and brings forth its emotion through verses like the powerful Wonder Woman, the enigmatic Angel Eyes and the lost hope in Cold.

It is a book that can be picked up and read in moments when you are lost or wondering how to go on, when you have a spare ten minutes on a commute to work or an hour at lunchtime.

Whatever time you have, it will be well worth spent and the words will last as long in the memory as they will on the page.

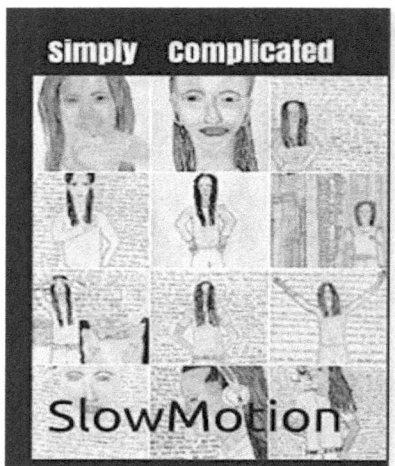

You can also check out coolgmack.com for books and merch

ABOUT THE SEXY AUTHOR

Coolgmack is more than a poet—he's a voice carved out of the concrete jungles of Westchester and NYC, the so-called "melting pot of ruin." Raised through group homes, jails, and institutions, he learned early that the streets can teach you just as much as any classroom—only harsher. After graduating from Sleepy Hollow High in '97, the pull of New York's darker corners dragged him into Rikers Island, robbing him of his prime but igniting the fire that would shape his destiny.

Years spent inside cages could have broken him—but instead, he chose to sharpen his words into weapons of truth. Poetry became his sanctuary, his megaphone, his redemption. While serving an unjust, perpetual sentence (smh), Coolgmack vowed to flip his pain into purpose. His verses carry the grit of survival, the ache of injustice, and the hope of transformation.

Today, he writes not just to heal himself but to uplift communities caught in the same cycle. His mission is unity, strength, and the reminder that your circumstances don't define your future. A poet, author, publisher, and entrepreneur, Coolgmack is on a mission to spark revolution through revelation—helping others uncover their inner talents and believe in more than the struggle.

You can find him everywhere the ink spills—Instagram, Facebook, Amazon, or at **coolgmack.com**. Step inside his books , including his latest drop *Sucker4Love Too*, and witness the holy fusion of pain, passion, and purpose.

www.ingramcontent.com/pod-product-compliance
Lightning Source LLC
Chambersburg PA
CBHW072155070526
44585CB00015B/1150